JOE
COOL

© UFS

THIS BELONGS TO
Mrs. Miller

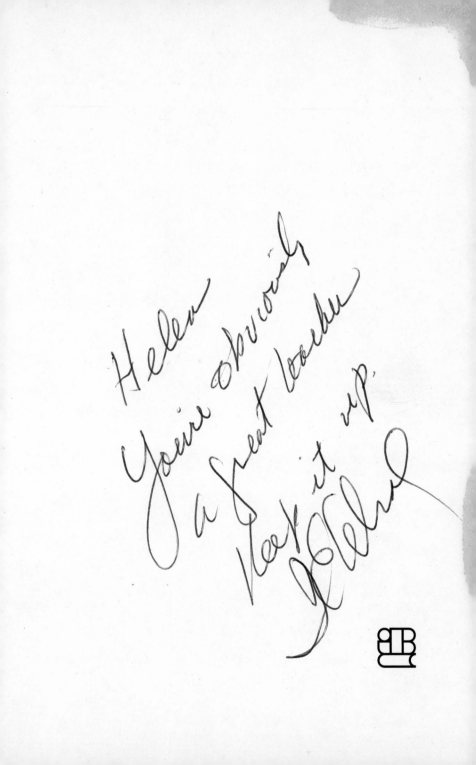

Helen
You're obviously
a great worker.
Keep it up.

Leading

with

Soul

Lee G. Bolman

Terrence E. Deal

Leading
with
Soul

An Uncommon Journey
of Spirit

Jossey-Bass Publishers • San Francisco

Substantial discounts on bulk quantities of Jossey-Bass books are available to corporations, professional associations, and other organizations. For details and discount information, contact the special sales department at Jossey-Bass Inc., Publishers. (415) 433-1740; Fax (800) 605-2665.

For sales outside the United States, please contact your local Simon & Schuster International Office.

Jossey-Bass Web address: http://www.josseybass.com

TCF Manufactured in the United States of America on Lyons Falls Turin Book. This paper is acid-free and 100 percent totally chlorine-free.

Library of Congress Cataloging-in-Publication Data

Bolman, Lee G.
    Leading with soul: an uncommon journey of spirit / Lee G. Bolman, Terrence E. Deal. — 1st ed.
        p.   cm. — (The Jossey-Bass management series)
    Includes bibliographical references.
    ISBN 1-55542-707-3
    1. Leadership—Moral and ethical aspects. 2. Leadership—Religious aspects. I. Deal, Terrence, E. II. Title. III. Series.
HD57.7.B64   1994
658.4'092—dc20   94-34348

Interior design and composition by Nancy Sayre Simerly
Illustrations by Barbara Rhodes

Credits are on page 195.

FIRST EDITION
HB Printing   10 9 8 7 6

For

Barry Edwin Deal   August 17, 1959 – November 28, 1964

Eldred Ross Bolman   March 3, 1914 – May 4, 1985

CONTENTS

CONTENTS

Leading
with
Soul

INTRODUCTION

Leadership and the Meaning of Life

All day I think about it, then at night I say it.
Where did I come from, and what am I supposed to be
doing?
I have no idea.
My soul is from elsewhere, I'm sure of that,
and I intend to end up there.

—*Rumi*

Soul. The word often sounds strange to modern ears. Terms like *heart* and *spirit* seem almost as exotic. We rarely think or talk about where we came from or what we are here to do. We need to. Otherwise, we deaden our souls, stunt our spirits, and live our lives halfheartedly. This book is about the journey to hope, faith, and heart. It is a guide to the path that leads from where we are to where we dream of being.

Our approach is ecumenical, embracing many spiritual sources: some secular, others religious. Our purpose is to apply wisdom and insights from diverse sources to the deeper, spiritual concerns of the modern manager. Though everyone needs a personal road to faith, the world needs a spirituality that transcends sectarian boundaries. Living in the global village inevitably means that cultures and faiths meet and interpenetrate at a dizzying pace. All too often, the tragic outcome is a collision of hatred and murder. Yet the basic spiritual teachings and moral precepts of the world's great religions are remarkably similar. Mahatma Gandhi said that he believed in the truths of all of them and that "there will be no lasting peace on earth unless we learn not merely to tolerate but even to respect the other faiths as our own. "[1]

In the workplace, all of us need a language of moral discourse that permits discussions of ethical and spiritual issues, connecting them to images of leadership. As management expert Elsa Porter puts it, "In a seminar with seventeen executives from nine corporations, we learned how the privatization of moral discourse in our society has created a deep sense of moral loneliness and moral illiteracy; how the absence of a common language prevents people from talking about and reading the moral issues they face. We learned how the isolation of individuals—the taboo against talking about spiritual matters in the public sphere—robs people of courage, of the strength of heart to do what deep down they believe to be right. They think they are alone in facing these issues. "[2]

Leading with Soul updates an ancient literary form. It is organized around conversations between a beleaguered leader and a wise sage, and it tells a story. Over the centuries, basic moral lessons have often been expressed through stories. Spiritual leaders of all traditions and faiths have taught and learned through example and dialogue. Christian and Sufi parables, Zen koans, the Jewish Haggadah, Taoist allegories, Hindu legends, and Native American tales are but a few examples. This legacy of wisdom, accumulated over many centuries, has provided much of the inspiration and ideas that infuse this book. The hope is that our work will kindle leaders' interest in spirituality as a way to make sense of perplexing riddles that technical knowledge cannot decode. In matters of ethics and spirit there may be nothing more practical than a good fable.

Fables embody our dreams. We all wish for a world of peace and security. We yearn for a Camelot: lives with purpose, efforts that make a difference, families filled with love, caring communities. Garrison Keillor, the creator of National Public Radio's "A Prairie Home Companion," echoes these longings in describing his mythical town of Lake Wobegon, "where all the women are strong, all the men are good-looking, and all the children are above average." How do we find such spiritual oases?

If we do not listen to the spirit within us, our deepest longings go unfulfilled. Self-doubt and cynicism eclipse confidence and hope. Our faith in technology's ability to cure our problems is waning. Dramatic technical breakthroughs took us to the moon. They put a microwave in almost every kitchen and instant dinners in every freezer. Yet when do we find time for family, for relaxation, or even for ourselves? Remote controls let us graze through dozens of television channels—everything from old movies to in-home shopping. Does this dazzling array satisfy our hunger for a richer, fuller, more meaningful life?

Technology continues to march ahead, yet chronic social and economic problems get worse. Communities suffer from levels of crime, chemical dependence, and alienation unprecedented in a civilized society. Families and children are in more trouble than at any time in recent memory. Many schools are ruled by gangs and ripped by violence. Children murder children. Has our contemporary emphasis on reason and progress put us on a one-way street to personal anguish and social disarray?

Our rational trajectory has failed to solve deepening problems in the workplace. Organizations scramble to downsize and outplace in the hope of avoiding extinction. Businesses lose market share to foreign competitors. Hospitals stagger under spiralling costs, erratic quality, and galloping bureaucracy. Schools are under fire for closing more minds than they open. Frazzled and exhausted managers scratch their heads, often contemplating escape or early retirement.

Many people hope that leadership will put us on a more promising path. But what kind of leadership? Here consensus evaporates. Two images dominate: one of the heroic champion with extraordinary stature and vision, the other of the "policy wonk," the skilled analyst who solves pressing problems with information, programs, and policies. But both images miss the essence of leadership. Both emphasize the hands and heads of leaders, neglecting deeper and more enduring elements of courage, spirit, and hope.

Perhaps we lost our way when we forgot that the heart of leadership lies in the hearts of leaders. We fooled ourselves, thinking that sheer bravado or sophisticated analytic techniques could respond to our deepest concerns. We lost touch with a most precious human gift—our spirit.

To recapture spirit, we need to relearn how to lead with soul. How to breathe new zest and buoyancy into life. How to reinvigorate the family as a sanctuary where people can grow, develop, and find love. How to reinfuse the workplace with vigor and élan. Leading with soul returns us to ancient spiritual basics—reclaiming the enduring human capacity that gives our lives passion and purpose.

Historically, humans have found meaning in work, family, community, and shared faith. They have drawn upon collective resources to do what they could not do alone. United efforts—raising a barn, shoring a levee, rescuing earthquake victims, or singing a hymn—have brought people together, created enduring bonds, and exemplified the possibilities of collective spirit. Such traditional sources of meaning, energy, and achievement are now seriously endangered. Many of us still go to church, temple, or mosque. Yet we often attend these religious services with the same attitude we bring to lectures, films, or rock concerts. We go as audience, as consumers of entertainment, not as passionate believers in a shared faith. Cultures with religion at their core build cathedrals and temples as symbols of faith. Our contemporary equivalents of liturgy and ritual are housed in shopping malls.

As God took a back seat, reason, science, and technology promised to answer life's challenges. Vaclav Havel, the writer and president of the Czech Republic, eloquently captures the limits of that promise:

> Classical modern science described only the surface of things, a single dimension of reality. And the more dogmatically science treated it as the only dimension, as the very essence of reality, the more misleading it became. We may know immeasurably more about the universe than our ancestors did, and yet it increasingly seems they knew something more essential about it than we do, something that escapes us. . . . Thus we enjoy all the achievements of modern civilization that have made our physical existence easier in so many important ways. Yet we do not know exactly what to do with ourselves, where to turn. The world of our experiences seems chaotic, confusing. Experts can explain anything in the objective world to us, yet we understand our own lives less and less.[3]

⁓

What has escaped us is a deep understanding of the spirit, purpose, and meaning of the human experience. How did this loss occur? In no small part, it happened because traditional religions had established their basic tenets to fit the conditions and the cosmology of the largely agrarian world in which people lived a thousand or more years before the rise of modern science and technology. In the wake of scientific revolutions like those of Copernicus and Darwin, religious leaders have been struggling to find plausible and compelling applications of ancient wisdom to modern lives. A fruitless battle has raged for decades: religious conservatives fight a rearguard battle against the advance of science while scientific imperialists reject any route to truth other than their own. The argument is pointless. It makes no more sense to rail against scientific progress than to hope that science can answer our spiritual questions.

Deep in our hearts, all of us need to find, or rediscover, a different path—to rekindle new meaning in both secular and religious organizations. But what is this different path? And where do we find the courage to follow it? The authors of this book know the fears firsthand. When we began, we were groping in unfamiliar terrain. On a ride to the airport in Kansas City, nine-year-old Chris Bolman asked his father, "Where are you going?"

Lee responded, "To San Francisco to work on a book with Terry."

"What's the book about?"

"It's about leadership and the meaning of life."

"Why are all your books about leadership?"

"I write about leadership and organizations because that's what I know about."

Chris unerringly zeroed in on the big question: "What do you know about the meaning of life?"

It was a question we had to face repeatedly. Experimenting with a new way to connect with readers on an uncommon journey is not easy. Nor is searching for new ways to infuse secular organizations with soul and spirit. Both are hard to talk about. They are elusive, ethereal, and subject to widely differing interpretations. Many doubt that they exist. Yet the more deeply we engaged questions of soul and spirit, the more convinced we became that they are at the core of people's lives as individuals and as members of communities.

Soul and *spirit* are often used interchangeably, but there is an important distinction. Following the lead of author James Hillman, we see soul as personal and unique—grounded in the depths of personal experience. Spirit is transcendent and all-embracing. It is the universal source, the oneness of all things: God, Yahweh, Allah, the Buddha. Soul and spirit are related in the same way as peaks and valleys, male and female. They are intimately connected. Each needs the other. Leaders with soul bring spirit to organizations. They marry the two, so that spirit feeds soul rather than starving it and soul enriches spirit rather than killing it. Leaders of spirit find their soul's treasure store and offer its gifts to others.[4]

Books about spirituality often speak from a specific religious tradition. That is not our objective. "Spirituality is the goal, religion is the path."[5] It is not the only path. The word *religion* describes a group of people bound by a vision of the divine expressed through shared beliefs, institutions, rituals, and artifacts. Every great religion offers special gifts, based on a unique spiritual tradition. Other paths fall outside established religion. Alcoholics Anonymous, for example, offers its widely respected, highly successful twelve-step program to help its members find meaning in a life without alcohol. AA's approach is explicitly spiritual, insisting that members place their trust not in themselves but a higher power. At the same time, individuals are free to interpret that power as they choose.

Take Randy Way,[6] one of many young Americans who became addicted to heroin in Vietnam. Back home, his life went from bad to worse. Close to suicide, he wound up in a psychiatric detoxification hospital. There, a fellow Vietnam veteran drew him into an AA-influenced program emphasizing spirituality and trust in a higher power. At first, Way rejected the entire concept: "My first thought to that was, I'm fucked. Here I am. If this is the only thing that works, I'm in trouble because none of this shit do I believe in."

But something finally got through to him:

> In the AA program, what they say is, "God as you understand him." So finally one day that clicked …as I understand him. Well the first thing is, I don't understand him. I don't know this guy. I have no idea. But I got the opportunity to work with some other people to where I was the teacher, so to speak, and I watched miracles happen in their lives—I mean, righteous miracles…. So if I gotta draw a line and say this is my belief, all I could say is there's somethin' happenin' that's a lot bigger than I am and it's a lot bigger than anybody I know.[7]

This book is about the search for something bigger. We hope it will speak to readers engaged in their own quest. Randy Way had a simple explanation of the importance of his encounter with spirit. Off drugs for six years, he discovered a simple truth: "When I do good, I feel good. There's nothing complicated about that. There's no books in the Bible that can make me feel like that. There's no drugs that can make me feel like that. If I do good, I feel good."[8]

Heart, hope, and faith, rooted in soul and spirit, are necessary for today's managers to become tomorrow's leaders, for today's sterile bureaucracies to become tomorrow's communities of meaning, and for our society to rediscover its ethical and spiritual center. Leading with soul requires giving gifts from the heart that breathe spirit and passion into your life and organization. Join us on a spiritual quest to look inward. Seek new sources of vigor, meaning, and hope to enrich your life and leave a better legacy for those who come after you.

The Search

CHAPTER 1

The Heart of Leadership Lives in the Hearts of Leaders

His name was Steven Camden. Like the city in New Jersey. He grew up in New Jersey, but in Newark, not Camden. Not that it made much difference. There were tough neighborhoods in both places. He had learned to survive in one of the toughest.

He was tired, and it was getting dark. He had just driven three hours up this mountain from the city. Why? He still wasn't sure. Why had John sent him? He climbed the fieldstone steps and knocked on the door. He waited. Was she here? She knew he was coming, didn't she? She must know that he had better things to do than just stand on her doorstep. He looked again and she was there.

Her name was Maria. He first noticed her eyes: deep, brown, full of something he recognized but could not name. They made her seem younger than he knew she was. Once inside, he looked quickly around the room. Mostly he noticed the Japanese art. It was like a gallery. But something was missing. What?

You've spent time in Japan, he said.

She nodded. Many years. Every piece is a memory.

I lived in Tokyo two years myself.

For him Tokyo had been an endless series of business meetings. No time for galleries. All his souvenirs came from the duty-free shop in the Tokyo airport.

She seemed to be waiting. Was he supposed to make the next

move? Where to begin? Blurt out his worries to a woman he barely knew? He tried to buy time. John seems to have a lot of confidence in you, he said.

We're old friends. I knew him back when he was starting your organization. We've become even closer since he retired. I've learned a lot from him.

She seemed to be waiting again. Now what? He'd always been good with words. Where were they now?

Do you feel uncomfortable here? she asked.

No. He hesitated. Well, maybe a little. Maybe I shouldn't have come.

Have some tea. He watched her pour the tea. He wanted coffee, but took the tea.

You've been working hard?

All my life. He sipped his tea. Green tea. Reminded him of Japan. He'd ordered it many times. *Nihon cha, kudasai.* A comforting sense of nostalgia.

Why? she asked.

Why what? He'd lost track.

Why do you work so hard?

He'd never thought about it. He paused. Why does anyone work hard? It's what you do. It's how I got where I am.

Do you like where you are?

Of course. He was lying. He knew it. Did she? Probably. Well, maybe not. Not as much as I used to.

What's changed?

He hesitated. Should he tell her the truth? What did he have to lose? He vaguely imagined John looking over his shoulder. I was promoted a year ago. They put me in charge of one of our subsidiaries. I was sure I was ready.

And now?

He stared at the cranes delicately circling the outside of his teacup. Until this job everything went right. Fast track. People seemed to think I could walk on water. Maybe it was talent, maybe luck, maybe just a lot of sweat. Whatever, it's not working any more.

You feel discouraged? She sounded sincere, maybe even caring. Why did she make him so nervous?

Like I'm on a treadmill. Running faster and faster. Getting farther and farther behind.

You need to get off.

I didn't need to drive three hours to learn that. I'm trying. He knew he sounded impatient. That's how he felt.

What have you tried?

Just about everything. Better time management. A mission statement. Strategic planning. Reengineering. Training. A quality program.

Why was she staring at him? Why so silent? Did she think he'd done the wrong things? That he hadn't done enough?

He continued. I sent executives to a management program. Top rating in *Business Week*. Hired consultants. World-class guys with world-class fees. I read *Fortune* and the *Harvard Business Review*. Talk to my boss.

She laughed. Why do you do all those things?

Her laughter grated. He felt his shoulders tighten. Was she laughing at him? It worked in the past. Why not now?

She turned serious. What do you want from me?

The question stung. What did he really want? He groped for an answer. His mouth felt dry. My work is my life. Always has been. What I always wanted. But a lot of the fun is gone. My boss is getting restless. It's the first time I ever felt I might fail in a job.

What's not working? she asked.

He told her about needing unity, but people's never agreeing. He said he needed a vision, but it was hard to see beyond next week. He told her he was lost. Things seemed to be falling apart. He'd never felt that way before.

She said she'd been there. That she understood.

Where had she been? Did she really understand? He wanted to say something. No words came.

And your spirit? she asked.

He looked to the door. He wanted to run. Get some fresh air. Get away from this crazy woman. Somehow he couldn't move. Spirit? he stammered.

Yes, your spirit. Her tone was firm, assured. As if it were a perfectly normal question. Was she serious?

What do you mean?

Spirit. The internal force that sustains meaning and hope.

He was squirming. Was it a mistake to come here?

A business is what you make it, she said calmly. If you believe it's a machine, it will be. A temple? It can be that too. Spirit and faith are the core of human life. Without them, you lose your way. You live without zest. You go through the motions, but there's no passion.

He was frustrated. He felt the anger building. He'd driven three hours for this? Through clenched teeth, he told her what he felt. Look, I'm running an organization, not a church.

Her eyes fixed on his. She smiled. What do you hope to run it with? More sweat? More control? More tricks and gimmicks?

Maybe some wisdom. He hadn't meant to say that, but it came out anyway.

Wisdom comes later. First you have to look into your heart.

He was squirming again. Embarrassed. He could feel the blood rushing to his face. Why was he still here? Why didn't he get up and walk out? You sound like my mother, he said scornfully. 'Follow your heart,' she always said. She never really understood business.

Do you? she asked.

Of course.

Then set a new course. You want to lead, don't you?

He nodded glumly. She continued.

The heart of leadership is in the hearts of leaders. You have to lead from something deep in your heart.

Like what?

I can't tell you what's in your heart, nor would you want me to. Would you want someone to offer you fruit but chew it up before giving it to you? No one can find meaning for you. Not your consultants, not your boss, not the *Harvard Business Review*. Only you really know what's in your heart.

He felt a twinge in his chest. A coincidence? He knew he'd been working too hard.

This isn't what you expected, she said.

Not at all.

It feels strange?

She was right. She seemed to know everything. Maybe a little, he admitted, wishing he hadn't.

She poured him more tea. You've been in uncomfortable situations before, haven't you?

Sure.

Have you learned from them?

He tried to review all his awkward moments. He gave up. There were too many. Usually, he said.

Good. Then, shall we continue?

Continue what? A senseless conversation? Still, she seemed to be onto something. Something he couldn't quite grasp. Maybe. I'm not sure.

Would you like some time to think?

A walk maybe.

Try the garden. We can talk more when you get back.

CHAPTER 2

The Human Heart is More than a Pump

The walk helped. A chance to clear his head. He'd been told she was good. Very good. But she wasn't making sense. Off in the ozone. Talk more, she'd said. About what?

He found her reading in her study. Look, he said. Heart and spirit can wait. I've got problems now.

She looked up from her book. Perhaps that's your problem.

His jaw tightened. He was tired of playing games. He spat out, Just what the hell are you talking about?

About you. She paused, looking at him. You're decisive. You get things done.

Yeah. She's starting to get it, he thought.

You think things through. You're a good analyst.

True.

You take charge. You're on top of things.

One of my strengths. He was feeling better now. She was beginning to understand him.

Maybe your biggest weakness.

Was this a trap? He hated weakness. He felt his face flush again. He could barely control his rage. Look, I'm a manager, not a social worker. You've got to be tough to get ahead.

How tough?

Why couldn't she get it? Put her in her place, then get out of here. I'd heard you could help. Obviously bad advice. You're off the mark. Wasting my time. You're . . .

She laughed gently. At him?

I'm sorry, he said. I don't mean to offend you. Why was he apologizing? She was the one to make amends.

Are you trying to scare me away? she asked.

She was right. She was getting too close. She'd triggered an old pattern. When he felt vulnerable, he went on the attack. Okay. I'm upset. Tired. I'm looking for help.

Maybe your head and hands have taken you as far as they can. Consider a new route. A journey of the heart. Your heart is more than a pump. It's your spiritual center. Heart is courage and compassion. Without it life is empty, lonely. You're always busy but never fulfilled.

He felt panicky, scared. He wanted to protest, but the words wouldn't come. Then it hit him. Right in the pit of his stomach. Maybe she was right.

You've had a long day, she said.

He nodded.

Get some rest. We'll talk more in the morning.

CHAPTER 3

The Journey of a Soul

The path curved gently up the mountainside. Above, a canopy of pine and spruce filtered the morning sun. Below, a blanket of wild flowers and a lake. Beautiful, he thought. The smells and sounds of spring surrounded them.

I love it here, she said.

I can see why. I should do this more often. He couldn't remember his last walk in the woods. Too little time. Too much to do.

If you let it, nature lifts your spirit. It touches your heart.

Spirit. Heart. Again. What was she talking about? A journey of the heart, he said. How about a road map?

It's an inward journey. There is no map. You find your soul by looking deep within. There you discover your spiritual center.

I was hoping for something more concrete.

How can I give you directions to your soul?

Are you a therapist?

No.

Some kind of religious nut?

She laughed. Does the word spirit scare you?

No, no. He was nervous. Puzzled. But not scared. There wasn't much that frightened him. It's just that I didn't come here for sermons. I want answers.

Have you been finding them?

No. That's why I'm here.

An old sage was once walking along a path very much like this one. Another man, not much younger than you, approached from the other direction. The young man's eyes were so riveted to the path that he bumped into the sage. The sage looked at the young man sternly, and asked him where he was going. 'To catch my future,' the young man replied. 'How do you know you haven't already passed it?' the sage asked.

He hated to admit it, but he saw a resemblance. He was like the young man in the story. You're talking about me?

Do you think so?

Eyes front. Tunnel vision. He was conceding more than he wanted.

She continued up the path. She didn't seem surprised. Same Mona Lisa expression. Same warm, soft tone.

A journey of the soul is a quest through uncharted territory. You find your way by opening your eyes. And your heart.

A ground squirrel scampered across the path. It seemed to know where it was going. Why didn't he? So where do I begin? he asked.

Where you are.

I'm not sure where that is.

That's a good beginning.

For what?

For your journey.

They came to a stream and sat down. They sat in silence, watching a leaf float past.

CHAPTER 4

Discovering New Teachers

See that leaf. It wends its way to wherever the stream is taking it, she observed.

Look, I'm not a leaf. He meant to sound forceful. I'm a manager. My job is to control things, not be controlled.

She moved closer. Looked directly at him. Her eyes felt penetrating. Are you succeeding?

Maybe not. Not anymore.

Control is an illusion. It's seductive because it gives a feeling of power. Something to hold on to. So it becomes addictive. It's hard to give up even when it's not working. You can't start a journey until you let go of habits holding you back.

Tell it to my boss. I'm paid to be in charge.

That's the illusion. Look again at the water going by. There is a story about a stream that flowed around many obstacles until it arrived at a desert. The stream tried to cross, but its waters disappeared into the sand.

What's this got to do with me?

Maybe you and the stream have something in common.

Such as?

In the past, you always got past obstacles. Now you have a desert to cross.

That's a stretch. But if the stream found any answers, fill me in. I haven't heard any since I got here.

She seemed to ignore his sarcasm. The stream heard a voice. It said, 'The wind crosses the desert. So can the stream.' The stream protested, 'The wind can fly but I cannot.' The voice responded, 'Let yourself be absorbed by the wind.' The stream rebelled. 'I want to remain the same stream I am today.' 'That is not possible,' said the voice. 'But your essence can be carried away and become a stream again. You've forgotten your essence.' The stream remembered dimly that she had once been held in the wind. She let her vapor rise into the arms of the wind, which carried the vapor across the desert and then let it fall in the mountains. There it again became a stream.

Evaporation won't work for me.

Probably not. But letting go might.

Letting go of what?

The defenses you're using to push me away. The mind-set that's got you stuck.

He looked away. He stared at the stream for several minutes. Let go. Of what? Of something he had clutched tightly for too long. He watched another leaf, trying to hold back the feelings welling up. They came anyway.

He spoke slowly, his voice cracking. In the story the stream remembered a time long before when the wind held it. Being held in the past. He hesitated, waiting for a wave of feelings to pass. I was five when my father died. Sweetest guy in the world. Never stayed in a job. Left me and my mom with nothing. We didn't talk about him much. The message was always, 'Don't be like him. Make something of yourself.'

Have you followed that advice?

It worked. At least I thought so. Maybe I have lost something.

Somewhere along the way.

You've lost touch with your soul.

If that's true, where do I look?

Inside. Outside. Your soul is inside, at your core. Teachers outside can help you find it.

Which teachers?

They're all around you.

Been to dozens of seminars. Workshops. Taught by top people. I didn't always learn that much.

Did any of them mention soul?

No. They usually don't. Not in management seminars.

She laughed. At least she had a sense of humor.

You're looking in the wrong places. she said. Life's deepest lessons are often where you least expect them.

Like the school of hard knocks.

Sometimes the lessons are very hard. I remember a man who met regularly with a group of friends. One day he said to his friends, 'I have discovered a new teacher. It's called AIDS.'

AIDS had hit Steve's old neighborhood hard. Maria's story cut deep. Beyond his usual defenses. He tried to dam the emotion coming from somewhere deep inside. Don't cry, he told himself. The tears came anyway. His face reddened with embarrassment. Why was he crying in front of this woman?

It's a powerful story, she said softly. His friends cried too. Their tears almost hid the real lesson. On life's journey, we pass guideposts every day. Mostly we don't notice. Tragedy is the author of hope. Crisis brings us face to face with our soul.

Soul. Journey. He spoke deliberately, pondering each word. A year ago I'd have been out of here when I heard those words.

And now?

Maybe I've found a new teacher.

Reclaiming Your Soul

Some say that my teaching is nonsense. Others call it lofty but impractical. But to those who have looked inside themselves, this nonsense makes perfect sense. And to those who put it into practice, this loftiness has roots that go deep.

—*Lao-tzu*

Like an exotic butterfly, spirit is elusive. Trying to capture it risks destroying it. Like the wind, spirit is invisible, yet you can still feel its presence and see its effects. Over the centuries, sages, philosophers, and ordinary human beings have reached for this powerful force just beyond their grasp.

Writing these first dialogues brought to our minds the words of an ancient Chinese philosopher: "I have just said something. But I don't know whether what I have said has really said something or whether it hasn't said something."[1] While convinced of the need to revive spirit in modern organizations, we know the challenge of trying to show others the nature of this journey.

We also know that Steve Camden's malaise is not uncommon. He is suffering what Albert Schweitzer once referred to as a "sleeping sickness of the soul."[2] Its symptoms are loss of seriousness, enthusiasm, and zest. When individuals live superficially, pursue no goals deeper than material success, and never stop to listen to their inner voices, they block their spiritual development. Steve Camden could be the prototype for Carl Jung's *Modern Man in Search of His Soul*.

Today's stressful and turbulent world compounds the risk of stunted souls and spiritual malaise. Managers try almost anything to stay current and achieve success. Sometimes their efforts are rewarded. Too often they and their organizations lose touch with their cores. As consultants and researchers, we have repeatedly found that managers' first response is to focus on the rational and technical features of any situation. Analyze. Plan. Change policies. Restructure. Reengineer. These are sensible responses to many business problems, but they miss another, deeper dimension. Our work has taught us that the symbolic, expressive facets of organizational life are at the heart of inspired leadership. Have we merely rediscovered *charisma,* the label often given to leaders endowed with mystery, magic, or a gift from the gods? Or are we on the brink of something deeper?

The signs point toward spirit and soul as the essence of leadership. There is growing consensus that we need a new paradigm to move beyond the traps of conventional thinking. In truth, we may need to rediscover and renew an old paradigm, one deeply embedded in traditional wisdom. Camden, our story's embattled leader, is lost. With the help of a spiritual guide, he is starting along another pathway. Instead of looking outside for specific answers, he needs to look inward for a deeper source of inner wisdom. In his First Epistle, John the Evangelist wrote of Jesus, "The spirit you have received from him remains within you, and you don't need to have any man teach you. But that spirit teaches you all things and is the truth."[3] The same message is found in many other spiritual traditions. In a parable from eighth-century China, a novice goes to Ma-tzu, a spiritual master, in search of the Buddha's teaching. Ma-tzu asks why the novice is seeking help from others when he already has the greatest treasure inside him. The novice asks what treasure Ma-tzu means, and Ma-tzu says, "Where is your question coming from? *This* is your treasure. It is precisely what is asking the question at this very moment. Everything is stored in this precious treasure-house of yours. It is there at your disposal, you can use it as you wish, nothing is lacking. . . . Why then are you running away from yourself and seeking for things outside?"[4]

Life in the late twentieth century creates many obstacles for all of us when we seek our spiritual center. An entrenched pragmatic orientation places a premium on technical logic. A widespread tendency to specialize and compartmentalize leads us to dichotomize work and play, male and female, career and family, thinking and feeling, reason and spirit. We relegate spirituality to churches, temples, and mosques—for those who still attend them. We shun it at work. To change this is far from easy. Steve is on the verge of a scary and potentially perilous existential journey. Early on, he relies heavily on Maria, his spiritual guide, for support and direction. Yet she continually resists his efforts to put her in charge. Instead, she reaffirms a message found in

almost every spiritual tradition. The message warns against trying to put someone else in charge of your spiritual journey.
Instead, recognize and trust the power within you.

Steve's quest will be filled with paradox because "spirituality
transcends the ordinary; and yet, paradoxically, it can be found
only in the ordinary. Spirituality is *beyond* us, and yet is in
everything we do. It is extraordinary, and yet is extraordinarily
simple."[5] Though he does not know it yet, Steve's task is to
reclaim and rekindle his spiritual center.

"It does not matter how long your spirit lies dormant
and unused. One day you hear a song, look at an object, or see
a vision, and you feel its presence. It can't be bought, traded,
or annihilated, because its power comes from its story. No
one can steal your spirit. You have to give it away. You can
also take it back."[6] However, taking it back is rarely easy. Steve
will find that reclaiming his spirit, and his soul, requires
uncommon courage.

Conviction

CHAPTER 5

A Place to Start

A month had passed. He was back on her doorstep. Waiting
again. His shoulders were slumped, his expression dour. He felt
his heart pounding. Where was she? Why was he back?
Something had pulled him here again. But what? Then she was
there. He felt better. At least she hadn't deserted him.

She led him to her study. Motioned him to a chair. He sat
down. Groped for words.

How are you doing? she asked.

Looking for insights. Waiting for a light bulb to go on.

And?

Nothing. Darkness. More confused than ever. He looked
down. He felt stupid.

That's good.

He was surprised again. Why?

You've begun your journey. At the start, confusion is to be expected.

But I feel lost.

You want everything planned in advance. That's fine for a trip to Chicago. It won't work for a journey of the spirit. First, you have to get started. Move into uncharted territory. Explore. Meditate. You'll know if you're on course.

How will I know? It feels scary.

Why? she asked.

I'm not sure.

Maybe something in the past?

Her question took him back in time. They sat in silence. He felt his body tighten as old memories floated to the surface. He wanted to push them back down, but they kept coming.

It's hard to talk about, he said.

Too scary?

No, he said emphatically, jolted by her question. Just things I haven't thought about in a long time. I got lost at a carnival once. I was panicked. Terrified. I still dream about it. Remember Hansel and Gretel? In new places, I still leave crumbs.

She was smiling broadly.

What's so funny? he asked.

I'm smiling because your story is so familiar. As a little girl, I used to play in a field next to our house. It was very hot one summer. Everything was very dry. I built a campfire, but it jumped over the ring of rocks I'd put around it. The whole field caught fire. It took the fire department two hours to put it out. I felt stupid. For a long time, I was terrified of doing the wrong thing again. I tried to avoid anything risky.

That's not what John says about you.

I've learned on my own journey. I wanted to find courage— like the Cowardly Lion in *The Wizard of Oz*. The Wizard says that everyone is afraid. Courage is the ability to go on anyway. It took me a long time, but I've learned to go on.

I want you to be my wizard. Give me the answers. You keep telling me to look inside. When I do, I hear the same voices. Be rational. Be in control. Be careful.

Those are messages from your head, not from your heart. It's hard to let go of old rules. It takes courage and faith.

Where do I find them?

You look for them.

Where?

You've asked that question before. Let's try getting to the answer a different way. She stood up and waved him over to a window. Those woods go on for miles. Take a walk. Get off the path. Explore. Make sure of one thing. Get lost.

Get lost? He stared at her in disbelief.

Exactly. Try it. See what happens.

I already know. I panic.

You think you know. You might discover something else. In the legend of the Holy Grail, each knight begins his search by entering the darkest place in the forest. No path. No guide. Try it.

He started toward the door. He hesitated. Old fears pulled at him, but he told himself he'd always been a risk taker. He turned around and forced a smile. Any crumbs to drop along the way?

They both laughed as he headed out the door.

CHAPTER 6

Vicissitudes of the Journey

It was getting dark. He was still lost, scrambling down a brushy slope. He never saw the branch until it slapped him in the face. It stung. His eyes watering, he sat down. He fought the panic. More memories swept over him. His father's death. His mother's breakdown. Living with grandparents. Working his way through college. Vowing to be successful. Getting what he wanted. Finding that success only brought more worries.

Much later, he found himself back at her house, enjoying the aroma of fresh coffee.

I was about to mount a search party. She smiled. Was she amused? Or relieved?

You told me to get lost.
I did.

Do you ever do anything halfway? Then she noticed the blood on his face. What happened?

Close encounter with a tree. It won.

Here. Let's clean it off.

It's nothing, he said.

Sit down! She spoke sternly. I'll be back in a minute.

He protested weakly. She ignored him and washed the scrape. Her touch was gentler than he expected. Close, her eyes were brighter, deeper. The feelings were almost too intense. He looked away.

I found a lake, he said. Walked around it a couple of times. Ran into more than the branch. Discovered things I buried long ago.

You can learn a lot walking around a lake.

When you were young, did you learn a prayer, 'Now I lay me down to sleep'. . . ?

She interrupted. 'I pray the Lord my soul to keep.'

The next line terrified me. Particularly after my father died. 'If I should die before I wake, I pray the Lord my soul to take.'

Do you still pray?

Not for years.

Why not?

Never seemed to make a difference. I stopped believing.

What do you believe in now?

I don't know. Maybe myself. Maybe nothing. A tone of resignation.

When you don't know what you believe in, you don't know who you are. You have no idea why you're here. You can't see where you're going. She spoke slowly, quietly. Every word emphasized.

I used to know where I was going. I got lost somehow.

Prayer is an avenue to faith. It's an intimate conversation with your soul. A heartsong.

A heartsong?

Your heart knows things that your mind cannot. Everyone needs a heartsong. It sustains you through the vicissitudes of the journey.

Vicissitudes? When had he last heard that word? In church? In the back of his mind a distant echo. She continued.

A spiritual pilgrimage always brings peaks and valleys. A heartsong sustains you along the way.

I remember sitting with my mother in a black church, he said. Music and singing. So much energy and intensity. Joy in the room. But spirituals are about suffering as well as happiness. They're a way to survive the pain.

Heartsongs carry us through both exhilaration and heartache. You've etherized your life to avoid the pain. At a price. If you wall off the valleys you close off the peaks as well. It's better to stop and sing from time to time.

Ether. Pain. More memories. His divorce. His children's suffering. An older son who never forgave him. The feelings would wait no longer.

He felt her touch—gentle, powerful, and accepting all at the same time. It helped him find the courage to face the pain he was feeling.

Fifteen years since my divorce, he said. My oldest son still doesn't answer my letters. The pain never stopped.

What did you do with it?

Ignored it. Threw myself into my work.

Did you talk to anyone?

A therapist. Nothing much happened. I was trying to get to something. Something deeper. I never found it.

Good therapists know the psyche. Great ones know the soul. People used to go to their priest or rabbi for spiritual guidance. Now where do they go?

Nowhere, I guess. Try to bury the feelings. Like I did.

Your divorce wounded your spirit. It's still not healed.

Is healing possible?

Yes. It's not easy, but it's possible.

How?

Tragedy enters every life. Spirit springs from what you make of it. Wounds provide an eye to find new possibilities.

He knew she was right. He remembered a story. I had a friend who wanted to be a champion rock climber. He got trapped in the mountains for a couple of days. Frostbite. Both legs amputated below the knee. He was determined to climb again. He got artificial limbs for climbing. Someone asked him how he could still climb so well. He laughed. He said now his calves didn't cramp.

Humor is a wonderful heartsong, isn't it?

I need to find my own.

Leaning into Your Fear

A good traveler has no fixed plans and is not intent upon arriving. A good artist lets his intuition lead him wherever it wants. A good scientist has freed himself of concepts and keeps his mind open to what is.

—Lao-tzu

Steve sought help when he became desperate. He hoped for specific solutions to immediate concerns. He resisted seeing that his outward problems were only symptoms of something much deeper. Slowly, he began to see that his real challenge was to come to terms with his soul. Maria became his guide.

Steve was victim to a widespread misconception that leadership expresses itself through individual heroism—waging war, championing a great cause, or single-handedly changing the course of history. In this view leaders' successes or failures are of their own making. They succeed if they have the right stuff—strength, courage, and vision. Failure is proof of their personal deficiencies. The archetypal image of this hero is the autonomous, lonely male wandering on the fringes of society—the Lone Ranger, Dirty Harry, or Rambo. This view taints our images of leadership. Would-be heroes, trying to emulate this image, often pay a heavy personal price: alienation, feelings of failure, stress-induced illness, and even early death.

Organizations and institutions suffer and sputter when we ask too much of our leaders and too little of ourselves. Effective leadership is a relationship rooted in community. Successful leaders embody their group's most precious values and beliefs. Their ability to lead emerges from the strength and sustenance of those around them. It persists and deepens as they learn to use life's wounds to discover their own spiritual centers. As they conquer their demons within, they achieve the inner peace and bedrock confidence that enable them to inspirit and inspire others.

The spiritual journey that leaders must take, and inspire others to take, begins *with* ourselves but not necessarily *by* ourselves. Maria told Steve to look both inside and outside because his quest will require both an internal exploration of soul and an external search for communion. To aid in the journey inward, every religious tradition has developed spiritual disciplines, or exercises. One is prayer, the "heartsong" that Maria offered to Steve. Others include meditation, studying scriptures, singing hymns, following prescribed rituals, journeying to sacred places, and contemplating nature. Similar practices have evolved independently in many different places and eras. There is a meditative tradition, for example, in almost every major religion, including Buddhism, Christianity, Hinduism, Islam, and Judaism.

The external journey is a search for collective spirit. Steve has found in Maria a spiritual guide who has found her way through a crisis much like his. He might have drawn support from a circle of friends, a spouse, close colleagues, or a religious community. But whatever the source of our external support, the first step we take toward enlightenment is an exploration of our inner being, a search for our existential core. Only then can we lead others.

Steve is learning to confront his fears—of letting go, of being out of control, of losing contact with comforting habitual anchors. He is embracing the ancient spiritual maxim that to hold too tightly to anything is to lose everything. As a seventh-century Zen master said, "The Great Way isn't difficult for those who are unattached to their preferences. Let go of longing and aversion, and everything will be perfectly clear."[1] The poet and visionary William Blake said it another way:

> He who binds himself to a joy
> Does the wingèd life destroy;
> But he who kisses the joy as it flies
> Lives in eternity's sunrise.[2]

Steve's conversations with Maria are helping him find the determination to move on. He cannot know in advance where his quest will lead. The decision to begin and the conviction to persevere will rest on his faith in the direction rather than fore-knowledge of the destination. The journey begins only when Steve's heart tells him that this is what he must do—even when reason and logic tell him otherwise. As he listens to his heart-song and finds the courage to answer its call, he embarks on an odyssey. As he continues, he will see things once invisible and do things once impossible.

Steve has lived his life in a safe zone, hoping to minimize uncertainty and to avoid pain. He now sees that his safe haven was a spiritual prison. "It is in passionate leaps of faith that we propel the human spirit forward. The safety of the known which only leads to boredom stifles the experience of life. As with heroes everywhere, the course of our lives may become a beacon to others who are on their own quests."[3]

History is full of stories of common people who do extraordinary things. In surmounting anguish and pain, they kindle their spirits and give strength to others. Our modern society encourages us to follow recipes or consult experts rather than find the fortitude to look inward. We buy diet books as a substitute for losing weight. We buy self-help books as an alternative to confronting our deepest fears and imperfections. We move from fad to fad without putting our heart fully into anything. It is not surprising that we feel powerless in the face of so many social and organizational ills. Beneath our helplessness is a spiritual vacuum. It saps our faith, weakens our heart, and leaves us foundering.

Bill Irwin provides a vivid example of what uncommon spirit can do. Excessive drinking left him blind by age twenty-eight.

In his early fifties, a recovering alcoholic, he decided to hike the entire 2,167 miles of the Appalachian Trail. His Seeing Eye dog was his sole companion. He faced daunting hazards—cliffs, storms, rough terrain, and his own fear—and endured the discomforts of primitive conditions, biting insects, and poison ivy. Before starting, he committed himself to the journey: "I don't care how many times I fall, I can always crawl to Maine."[4] Eight months later, he became the first blind person to walk the length of the trail. How did he do it? "He never saw the trail. He just took it. He did not stick to the plan others preconceived for the life of a blind man. He sought his own course, the one his spirit needed to follow."[5]

Embedded in Bill Irwin's story are dual messages of human imperfection and human transcendence. Irwin's youthful foibles led to his blindness. But he embraced a maxim that offers an alternative to the shallow optimism of the 1960s and the deep pessimism of the 1980s and 1990s. It says, "I'm not okay, and you're not okay. But that's all right."[6]

Paradoxically, in accepting our imperfections, we develop the conviction we need to embark on a necessarily ill-defined search for a better place. We also realize that the end of one quest is a prologue to the next. Ernest Becker, author of the Pulitzer Prize–winning book *The Denial of Death,* observed that man is the god who shits.[7] That paradox cuts to the heart of spirituality. To deny our imperfections is to reject our humanity and to become disconnected from our soul. The leader who falters, like the god who shits, is a paradox that only spirit enables us to accept and embrace.

A preacher once asked a group of children, "If all the good people in the world were red and all the bad people were green, what color would you be?" One girl thought for a long time, looking very serious. Then her face brightened, and she said, "Reverend, I'd be streaky."[8] We're all streaky. Acceptance of fear and imperfection and a willingness to undertake the journey of discovery anyway transport us to life's deepest core, "the inner value, the rapture that is associated with being alive."[9]

Gifts

CHAPTER 7

Gifts of Leadership

Late November. Gloomy sky. Chilling rain. As he trudged up the path, he could see her watching him through the window. His pace was brisk. His face told another story. Frustration. Gloom. Something unfinished.

After their brief pleasantries, she got to the point. You seem disappointed.

Yes and no. Ups and downs. Sometimes I'm soaring. It's like a great adventure. Mistakes don't drag me down so much. You were right about prayer. It helps.

You're finding heartsongs.

Particularly from Gwen.

Gwen is special to you?

I've asked her to marry me.

Has she agreed?

Not yet. But she's got me going to church on alternate Sundays. I'd been away too long. I'd forgotten the power. The prayers. The music. The liturgy. The feeling of community.

What about the other Sundays?

We take walks around a lake. We talk. We listen to the wind in the trees. Lunch in the same meadow each time. If you look you find reverence and ritual in nature.

She nodded.

He scanned the room. Suddenly it hit him. No photos, he said.

What?

No photos. First time I came, I knew something was missing. Beautiful art. But no friends. No family. No people anywhere.

He thought he saw something different in her eyes. Turmoil? Sadness? Quickly it was gone.

The art is enough, she said.

Was she telling the truth? Hiding something? Was he too intrusive? Avoiding his own struggles again?

She moved on, seeming to ignore his unstated question. You were saying mistakes don't bother you as much.

He suspected she was changing the subject. But why? He decided to let it go. Not as much. I'm clearer about what's important. But it's hard to express.

Why?

When I mention spirit, other people look at me like I'm an alien.

Everyone?

Not Gwen. She understands. So do a few of my friends. No one at work.

What happens there?

I'm their boss. They're careful. I can feel it. See it in their eyes. For example, I've been trying to drum up support for a weekly 'spirit breakfast.' Right now, I'm not sure anyone would come. I feel like a band leader who turned left at a fork. The rest of the band turned right.

You're trying to lead, but no one's following.

A drum major strutting solo.

Steve, you're discovering one of life's most precious gifts—the treasure of human spirit. You need to share it. You lead with soul by giving to others.

Leaders are supposed to give direction, he said.

What if I had directed you to seek your soul?

He paused, taking a moment to cover his embarrassment. I'd
have left. I wanted to anyway. Maybe it's the same with people
in my organization. Sharing spirit sounds good. But how?

With gifts.

Gifts?

Look at any of the great spiritual traditions. You find two
moral precepts at the core. Compassion. Justice. Are they at the
heart of your organization?

I wish they were.

You build them through offering gifts.

What gifts?

Four in particular. They emerge from two basic dualities: yin
and yang, matter and spirit.

Dualities? He meant to sound skeptical.

Opposites that make each other possible.

What was she talking about? Like no pain, no gain?

Well said. Opposites in harmony. The four gifts provide balance.

No question, my organization could use some balance.
But how...

From yin, viewed traditionally as the female principle, caring
and compassion—the gift of love. From yang, customarily seen
as the male principle, autonomy and influence—the gift of

power. From matter, the pragmatic world, accomplishment and craftsmanship—the gift of authorship.

And the fourth?

Later. When you're ready.

He felt a surge of anger. Come on! Was he a child? He didn't need to be spoon-fed.

She seemed to sense his anger. Impatience only slows your journey, she said.

She's been right before, he told himself. All right, he said. Start with the last one. Tell me about authorship.

It's the feeling of putting your own signature on your work. It's the sheer joy of creating something of lasting value. The feeling of adding something special to our world.

That's where I've been concentrating. We've been pushing hard on our World-Class Quality program. Getting our people focused on excellence. Producing something they can be proud of.

Are you satisfied with the results?

Not really. The harder I push, the more they seem to push back.

For instance?

We had a meeting last week to talk about why we're behind schedule on the quality program. I told people we'll never build a sense of responsibility if we keep missing deadlines.

You see the paradox. You hope they will become what you think they are not. You're trying to get them to accept something that you don't think they want.

I'm just trying to motivate them to do their best. Isn't that leadership?

Do you motivate a rosebush to blossom? Can you impel your children to grow? When you push people to become what they are already becoming, you get in the way. You become a meddler.

He felt the blood rise to his face. His throat tightened. His voice rose. Didn't you just say to give people authorship? That's precisely what I'm trying to do! How else am I supposed to get them to set higher standards?

Why do Zen masters teach that if you meet the Buddha on the road, kill him?

His brow knitted in puzzlement. Why did she keep answering questions with questions? What was she trying to tell him? He looked down at the floor. He kept looking for a connection. Finally it came. Because answers aren't outside. They're inside. I'm asking you when I already know the answer. He glanced out the window. The weather is lousy. Still, it's a good time for another walk.

He started down the steps. Still raining. Cold. Windy. Should he turn around? No, he wanted time to himself. He closed his raincoat and plunged forward.

CHAPTER 8

Authorship

He cut the walk short. Too cold.

She handed him a drink. Here's something to take the chill off.

The fifth gift—coffee, he replied.

She laughed. He sipped the dark brew. No cranes. Just a simple beige mug.

You were right, he said.

About what?

Shipping my question back to me, he continued. I wanted you to do my work. You wouldn't. I had to create my own composition.

Did you succeed?

I realized something. I was doing to you what people at work do to me all the time.

What's that?

Upward delegation. Dumping stuff in my lap.

Why?

Collusion. I love being the guy who solves the tough problems. They know I love it. They give me what I want.

It's a great way for you to stay busy.

Swamped. Chronically. With everyone else's work. They're off the hook. Protected from making mistakes. And from learning. Meanwhile, I never have time for the big picture.

It's the curse of the American leader. Particularly for men.

What curse? A trace of annoyance. Is male bashing a part of the program?

No. But rugged individualism is deep in the American psyche. Remember Gary Cooper in *High Noon*? The leader saves the day all by himself while the townspeople cower in the background. It's an endemic cultural message: 'If you have a problem, hope for a hero to rescue you.'

And blame the hero if things don't work out, he added. The rest of us feel we're not responsible. It's the leader's job to solve our problems.

It's different in Japan, she said. There it's the group's job to solve the leader's problems.

I had a similar thought on my walk. I read once about two oil company executives. Both had the same problem—a fire in a refinery. The American exec got a call at home. Rushed in. Met with his people. Got reports from the scene. Gave orders. A frantic morning of fire fighting.

A lovely example of the American way at work.

The Japanese executive arrived in his office. He sipped a cup of tea. Relaxed. Read the newspaper. Reviewed reports. Thought about strategy in the Middle East. Learned about the fire after it was under control. Subordinates explained how they had handled it. He congratulated them.

The Japanese know about the gift of authorship, she replied.

Maybe Japanese executives enjoy life more than I do. I always thought I was good at delegating. Clear about expectations. Good follow-up. But the buck still stops with me.

So your people don't feel a sense of authorship.

Hell, no. They're always looking over their shoulders. Trying to figure out what I want. Then I complain that they don't take responsibility. Vicious cycle.

Where no one wins.

If they succeed, I take credit. If they fail, I blame them. The crazy thing is that I put in a motivation program. Trying to persuade them of what they probably want to do anyway—if I'd just get out of the way.

It's a classic pattern. You're the parent and they're the kids. You shield them from responsibility. They look to you for direction and security.

They know I have the final say. Review everything they do. Why give me their best? They know I'll change it anyway.

On that short walk, you got a lot done. She was smiling.

More than you think. I jumped ahead. Started to think about the gift of love.

How far did you get?

Not very. It felt like thin ice. I stayed close to home. Started with Gwen. I love her. I know that deep in my heart. I wish I could express it better. I need to understand love as a gift.

What's happening with you and Gwen?

Good things. But hard to talk about. Why was she asking? She must have a reason. She always did.

I'm glad. Keep giving. You'll learn with practice.

And if I meet the Buddha?

Love him. You're making headway, she laughed. You may not even need me much longer. She walked him to the door.

He said good-bye. He wanted to say more. Why did she say he might not need her? Was she pushing him away? He didn't want that. Not yet.

CHAPTER 9

Love

It was February. Freezing. A driving rain beat against his windshield. The forecast promised snow in the mountains. He liked driving in snow. It softened things. Nothing to interrupt his solitude. A chance to think.

He thought about love. What made that word so powerful? He could talk about love with Gwen. Sometimes with his children. Never at work. Who talks about love in a corporation? You talk about it at weddings. Six months until the wedding. Gwen had finally said yes. Maybe the only love he really felt sure about.

Two months until his trip to Singapore. A new acquisition there. Great company. A merger is a little like a wedding, he thought. Two different companies. We can learn from them if we don't strangle them. That's the danger: we own you, so do it our way.

That's the connection. Same problem with Gwen. They had their biggest fights when he tried to make her more like him. Yet he loved her because she wasn't like him. Loving her meant treasuring who she is. The same with the acquisition. It's got to be mutual.

Whiteout. Snow so heavy he couldn't see past the wipers. He pulled off the road. Turned off the ignition. Silence. He *loved* nights like this. But the gift of love is something even deeper. More spiritual. He smiled at the thought of spirit. It wouldn't have occurred to him before he met Maria.

He heard snowplows. Droning. Clanking. As they passed he pulled in behind.

Well after midnight he arrived. The snow had stopped. The sky was clearing quickly. He saw a light in her study—she was waiting. He had hoped she would be.

He paused to look at the night sky. Dark patches of clouds giving way to stars. The moon almost full. In the past on nights like this the sky seemed to speak of cosmic comedy. Tonight it spoke to him of love.

You must be exhausted, she called from the front porch.

He was surprised. A departure from the routine—he didn't have to wait for her to come to the door.

Physically, yes, he called back. Spiritually, never better.

He came in. A mug of coffee was waiting.

I was starting to worry, she said.

No need to. I've been driving a long time. Had to stop once. Almost a total whiteout. Couldn't see a thing.

What did you do?

Pulled off. Watched the snow. Thought about love.

What happened?

A team of snowplows came along. I followed them.

That wasn't my question.

I know. He looked at her. You've given me love since the first time we met.

He wasn't prepared for her reaction. She glanced away momentarily, but said nothing.

He continued. I didn't understand love. I thought it was just attraction and desire. Like a business deal: you invest in the hope of a big return. That's not it.

She stood up. Let's talk more tomorrow. Even if you're not tired, I am. If you're hungry, try your luck in the refrigerator. How about we meet at eight?

He nodded assent.

We'll take a walk before breakfast, she added. It should be beautiful. She turned away.

See you in the morning, he responded.

He was puzzled. When he mentioned love, she seemed to pull back. He poured more coffee. He wandered around the house. All this art. No photos of people. She's so intense but always composed. What's behind her mask? Is she afraid of something? Is that why she lives up here alone?

By morning the sunlight dazzled on the new snow. Maria was her usual self. Warm. Confident. Inscrutable. He wanted to ask about last night. He decided to start on safer ground.

How do I give love in my organization? he asked as they walked along.

She smiled. He watched her breath form a translucent cloud in the icy air. In Japan some executives spend time every week cleaning out the toilets. It's part of their gift.

I'd try that, but people are already looking at me a little funny.

How *do* people know you care? she asked.

They probably don't. Particularly now. We had to lay people off last month.

How did you do it?

We did everything. Gave them plenty of notice. Supervisors met with everyone who was affected. We paid for counseling. Hired an outplacement service.

Did you talk to them yourself?

No. They're three or four levels down. Most of them I don't know.

Aren't you their leader?

He paused and scanned the snow-covered landscape. See the branches sinking under the weight of the snow? he asked.

Yes.

That's how I feel at work. Drooping under the burden. Like I've given all I can. There's not enough to go around.

You've got it turned around, she said. Maybe you're burdened because you haven't given enough.

Not as much as the Japanese executives. By that standard, I haven't shown people that I care about them.

Do they care about you? she asked.

Never really thought about it. Caring about the boss isn't in the job description.

Do you think love is a one-way street? Why didn't you talk to the people who were laid off? Look them in the eye. Give them comfort. Show them you understood.

I was busy, he protested half-heartedly. I didn't want to undermine the chain of command.

Those sound like lousy reasons.

Okay. Maybe I was afraid to face them. So I let someone else do it.

If you show people you don't care, they'll return the favor. Show them you care about them, they'll reciprocate.

An old message. When you give love, you get it back.

Sounds so simple that a lot of people don't believe it. The costs are subtle, hard to pin down. Most managers never notice what they're losing. When people know that someone really cares, you can see it. It's there in their faces. And in their actions. Love really is the gift that keeps on giving.

The opening he was looking for. Then why, he asked, did you reject my gift last night?

I was touched, but I wasn't expecting it. You were offering me something I wasn't ready for just then.

Was I getting too close?

No, you were moving too fast. It was the timing.

Timing. An old lesson. Always in a hurry. He'd tried to rush her. Pin her down. She wasn't rejecting his offer. But she wouldn't be caught up in his urgency. He had more to learn.

He thought back to his organization. With the people we laid off I missed the moment. But I can still do something with the people who stayed. I need to get out to Topeka. Singapore too. I've started on the road to giving authorship. I need to learn more about love as a gift.

Remember one thing, Steve. Everyone's different. A big part of love is caring enough to find out what really matters to others.

I haven't been doing that enough. Not last night. Not in my organization. I need to. It's scary. Opening my heart to people around me. I won't clean the office toilets tomorrow. I'll find my own way.

CHAPTER 10

Power

A dazzling spring day. More than a year since they first met. Perennials lining the way to her door. He laughed as he remembered his first visit. He'd been so frightened and lost. Nothing like the joy he felt at seeing her again.

How was Singapore? she asked.

Tough. Even tougher than expected. But it came out all right.

What happened?

I tried to show them I cared. My gift to them.

Were they looking for love?

No. Not at first. Lots of polite smiles. But you could feel the chill. They had a reception. I gave a little speech. Talked about caring. It flopped.

How did you know you missed the mark?

Arms crossed, blank faces everywhere.

Then what happened?

I got out on the factory floor. One of the workers, a young guy with a big, earnest smile, asked me to take a turn on his machine. I didn't have much choice. Big crowd circled around. I felt like a lamb circled by hungry wolves. I was fumbling all over the place. People thought it was hilarious.

And they loved you for it?

Just being out on the floor was the big thing. Talking to people. Saying hello. Answering questions. It was like I passed a test. On the way out, I met this woman. Maybe fifty years old, Chinese, tough looking. Came up and threw her arms around me. Told me everyone figured all I cared about was money. Now she says, 'We have a friend in America.'

How did you feel?

When a factory worker in Singapore gives you a hug, that's pretty amazing.

Love worked for you. She smiled. Every group creates a testing ground. It's like a sacred space that most of us never know is there. When you enter it and give from your heart, people know that you care.

Whatever worked in Singapore backfired in Topeka.

What happened there? she asked.

Timing was bad. Six months after the layoffs. I knew it would be tough. But I worked in Topeka my first job out of college. I thought we were still family.

Sounds like a risky assumption.

I found that out. There's this big guy, looks like he could have been a linebacker in the NFL. Runs a forklift. Abrasive as hell. Anyway, as soon as I get there, he's in my face, screaming. I'd fired his friends. Now I come in pretending we're one big happy family. Tells me I'm a phony. Like all those other big shots with big salaries.

That must have stung.

Remember that tree limb? This was even worse. Torture. How would you feel, hanging out there?

I've been there. I know. It's no fun.

It got worse. They knew how to twist the knife. End of the day, I was battered. Sat in the hotel room, nursing a glass of wine. Feeling sorry for myself. Wanting to hide. Just wanting out of there.

That's when you called me, isn't it? You woke me up.

It wasn't that late. Thought you'd be awake.

I wasn't feeling well that evening.

I'll call earlier next time. Are you okay?

There's a lot of stuff going around this year.

You helped me see that I'd brought the wrong gift. Bad timing again. I was offering love. They were saying bullshit, why'd you fire our friends? They weren't looking for caring. Not from me. They really wanted power.

She laughed. You dug yourself in pretty deep. Did you ever get out?

Not before I ate a lot of dirt. Next day we had this meeting. Old conference room in the plant. Cramped, bare walls, fluorescents, formica table, metal folding chairs. Martha Mendez, the union head, and her executive committee on one side of the table. Me and the plant manager on the other. They're mad. I'm scared. Mendez lays it all out. Rakes me and management over the coals. I'm biting my tongue so hard it bleeds.

It sounds pretty brutal. Have the scars healed?

They're healing. I sat there. Listened, asked questions. Told them I got the message: they felt betrayed. Management had been talking about listening, participation, empowerment for a long time. Then when something big came along we got amnesia. 'You admit you blew it?' Mendez asks.

How did you respond?

I barely got the word out, but I said yes.

You were pretty far out on a limb.

Fifty feet up from a rock quarry and Mendez was revving up her chain saw. I promised two things. Next time, I said, we'll listen. And we'll work with you to make this plant successful.

Layoffs are bad for credibility. Did they believe you?

No, not at first. But a couple of weeks later I got invited back. Some workers and managers had banded together to develop some proposals. They did their homework. Gathered data. Called other plants. Worked through some conflict. Got to consensus on what needed to happen. Some of it needed support from headquarters. It was another test, I guess. I almost flunked.

How?

One worker threw a half-baked idea in the hopper. No way we could spend that kind of money without a more careful look. I almost told him flat out it was a dumb proposal. Then I bit my tongue and thought hard. I asked him to lead a group to study it further. He was beaming.

It sounds like a good move. Caving in doesn't empower

people. You set a good example. You went to the plant. You listened. You were open.

Some of their ideas were terrific. Easy to say yes to. That night Mendez invited me over to her house for a barbecue. The whole union executive committee was there. Best team-building session I ever saw.

What did you learn?

You can give power away and wind up with more. You remember the old gasoline ad? I always thought power was like the tiger in the tank. You don't want to let the tiger out, you just let people hear him roar.

Hoard power, dampen spirit.

That's what I learned in Topeka.

CHAPTER 11

Significance

He was surprised, troubled when she opened the door. The gray in her hair and lines in her face had always been there. But not the first thing you noticed. Was she tired? Sick? Her face gave no other clue. Her eyes and her smile were as mysterious as ever.

She motioned him in. There's hot coffee.

He thanked her. Notice the headline this morning? Another young movie star dead. ODed on drugs.

She nodded. She seemed to understand. Why didn't he?

How can you have it all and have nothing? he asked.

Do you remember yourself when we first met?

Was she baiting another hook? She kept him alert, anyway. Forced him to think. You're right. The higher I climbed, the less it meant.

You felt insignificant.

Meaning what?

Meaning you were hollow at the core. No soul, no spirit, nothing.

How about some credit for progress?

Do you want to talk about the past or the future?

Maria, you are the most demanding, infuriating . . .

She interrupted and gestured toward the door. It caught him by surprise. You called this meeting. You can leave whenever you want.

Leave! I just drove three hours to get here. He paused, and laughed at himself. Not even an E for effort?

She laughed too. She must have known how he would react. How's your spirit? she asked. Her tone was gentler.

I remember the first time you asked. I figured you weren't playing with a full deck. It didn't make any sense. Now, it makes a lot.

You've made progress. But it sounds as if something else is on your mind.

The fourth gift. You never told me what it was.

I don't need to. You already know.

And?

What were we just talking about?

About how infuriating you are.

Before that, remember?

The movie star who died. Having it all and having nothing. Feeling insignificant.

Why not start there? she asked.

I did feel insignificant. Not now. Things are starting to make sense. He paused, grasping for the right word. Significance! That's what the fourth gift is about. Why hadn't he seen that before? Then it hit him. That's what you've given me.

Now, you can give it to others.

How?

Do you want me to do your work? You know about authorship. It's your organization. What comes to mind?

Times when I've felt significant. Maybe what works for me will apply to my organization.

Keep going.

Like my visit to Singapore. It was like being present at a birth. Coming together to generate something new. The power of shared emotion. Creating a common spirit that touched everyone.

How did it happen?

Maybe magic. Maybe love. I'm not sure. We prepared—a lot. Everyone knew the script, even though it wasn't written down. It still felt very spontaneous.

That's how good rituals feel.

Bad ones can backfire, though. My lesson in Topeka began as a disaster. I thought I was Santa Claus bringing gifts. They thought I was Scrooge taking away their friends.

What did you learn from that experience?

You can't impose significance. People have to create it together.

Exactly. Significance comes from working with others, doing something worth doing, making the world better. After that, you confirm the feeling and deepen it.

How?

With celebrations.

Celebrations?

Memorable events for special occasions. Ceremonies that only happen a few times a year. They connect people to a deeper, spiritual world. Celebrations weave our hearts and souls into a shared destiny. It's how people summon spirit, They come together to mark beginnings and endings, triumphs and tragedies, births and deaths.

We don't do that enough in my business.

Nor in most. So you lose the spiritual glue that holds people together. Think about religion. What are the ties there that bond people to one another?

You know the Emerald Buddha? he asked.

In Bangkok. I remember it vividly.

The faithful come to pray every day. The King of Thailand visits three times a year to change the Buddha's clothes. Fit the costume to the season.

For me it's a place of great reverence, she said.

Like the Cathedral of Notre Dame in Paris. I remember standing there in awe. The architecture, candles, statues, paintings of the saints, figures of Mary and Jesus. A group of visiting nuns sang a hymn, *a cappella*. Spontaneously. It took my breath away. Two feelings at once. I was soaring and going deeply into my own soul while at the same time joining with the souls of others.

That's the power of spirit. It fuses place, music, art, souls. It enfolds the everyday world in rapture and mystery.

Another memory. Some friends once invited me to their son's bris. As the ceremony began, the father sat holding his son. His father stood behind him. Afterward, I saw tears welling up in the grandfather's eyes. He told me that standing behind his son and grandson, he felt the presence of his own father and grandfather. The eternal human chain. Right there. I felt cheated. No one did much to mark special moments in my life. We went through the motions, but the spirit wasn't there.

Does your company mark special occasions?

He knitted his eyebrows as he thought for a moment. Not enough. We're cheating ourselves.

Do you tell stories?

What kind of stories?

Take this conversation. I asked you about spiritual bonds. You told stories. The Emerald Buddha. Your visit to Notre Dame. Memories of a bris.

A light bulb flashed. When you first talked to me about spirit and heart, I had no idea what you were talking about. You told stories. Parables. The stream that wanted to cross the desert. The young man too focused on his path to see anything else.

Stories take us to other worlds. They transport us to the world of spirit.

That's hard to buy if you grew up worshipping at the altar of facts and logic.

We're all flooded with facts and detail. More than we can handle. The flood of information keeps rising, and the world seems more and more out of control. Turn on the evening news. What do you see? Murders, political gridlock, trouble somewhere halfway round the world. It's confusing. Discouraging. Then you visit Notre Dame. Or you attend a bris. You feel clearer about what you're here to do and why it all makes sense.

Spring flowers were everywhere as he walked to his car. Maybe it's there in the flowers, he thought. He remembered a Zen story. The Buddha preached a sermon by lifting up a flower. The meaning in the flowers is that they're there, he thought. And my meaning is that I'm here. I'm alive.

On the drive home, he was flooded with questions about how to infuse his organization with significance. He laughed. He remembered how often the possessive pronoun *my* had got him in trouble in the past. For people to feel significant, he knew the organization had to be 'ours,' not 'mine.'

Community and the Cycle of Giving

Find the real world, give it endlessly away
Grow rich, fling gold to all who ask
Live at the empty heart of Paradox
I'll dance there with you, cheek to cheek

—*Rumi*

Leading is giving. Leadership is an ethic, a gift of oneself. It is easy to miss the depth and power of this message. The dialogues are intended to encourage readers to deepen their internal journey in search of the gifts they can offer to others.

The essence of leadership is not giving things or even providing visions. It is offering oneself and one's spirit. Material gifts are not unimportant—the gift of self will often take material forms. But what we have all heard is true—the most important thing about a gift is the spirit behind it. When Steve approached gift giving as a material transaction, he failed. When he offered his inner soul, he set in motion a reciprocal process—others gave of themselves in return. Gifts of authorship, love and caring, power, and significance only work when they are freely given and freely received. When the spirit is right, gift giving transforms an organization from a place of work to a way of life.

Your quest as a leader is "a journey to find the treasure of your true self, and then [to return] home to give your gift to help transform the kingdom—and in the process your own life. The quest itself is replete with dangers and pitfalls, but it offers great rewards: the capacity to be successful in the world, knowledge of the mysteries of the human soul, the opportunity to find your unique gifts in the world, and to live in loving community with other people."[1]

Authorship, love, power, and significance are not the only gifts that leaders offer. Any gifts will work, so long as they affirm the fundamental moral precepts of compassion and justice. Fused with soul and spirit, gifts form the cornerstones of a purposeful and passionate community. Leaders must discover for themselves the contributions that are theirs to make. We will elaborate here on the four gifts that Steve learned from Maria.

The Gift of Love

Pressures of immediate tasks and the bottom line often crowd out personal needs that people bring into the workplace. Every organization is a family, whether caring or dysfunctional. Caring begins with knowing about others—it requires listening, understanding, and accepting. It progresses through a deepening sense of appreciation, respect, and ultimately, love. Love is a willingness to reach out and open one's heart. An open heart is vulnerable. Accepting vulnerability allows us to drop our masks, meet heart to heart, and be present for one another. We experience a sense of unity and delight in voluntary, human exchanges that mold "the soul of community."[2]

Love has probably received more attention than any other human emotion. It has many meanings. Plato called it divine madness.[3] The medieval French troubadour Guiraut de Borneil saw its more tender side:

> Love is born, who its fair hope
> Goes comforting her friends.
> For as all true lovers know, love is perfect kindness
> Which is born—there is no doubt—from the heart
> and eyes.
> The eyes make it blossom; the heart matures it
> Love, which is the fruit of their very seed.[4]

Love is largely absent in the modern corporation. Most managers would never use the word in any context more profound than their feelings about food, films, or games. They shy away from love's deeper meanings, fearing both its power and its risks. So it was with Steve. In Topeka, he tried to minimize his risk and liability. Only by accepting anguish and vulnerability —the companions of love—could he offer a gift that was both accepted and appreciated.

The Gift of Authorship

Authorship is rare in most organizations. Though it may sound like a caricature, the old management approach was simple. Give people jobs. Tell them what to do. Look over their shoulders to make sure that they do things right. Reward or punish them depending on their performance. This approach was frustrating for everyone. Workers felt overcontrolled, underinformed, and undervalued. Even when they knew how to do the job better than their boss, they felt compelled to follow orders, often at the expense of performance. Disappointed superiors blamed workers for poor results and tightened supervision further. This constricting spiral undermined workers' sense of connection, ownership, and pride.

Despite efforts across corporate America to increase employee participation and enhance the quality of work, tens of thousands of people still see their work as just a job—they put in time, go through the motions, and collect a paycheck. Around the world, employees have developed similar levels of cynicism. A few years ago, Soviet workers elegantly captured such sentiments in the aphorism, "We pretend to work and they pretend to pay us." A similar cynicism has developed in recent years among many African-American adolescents. Viewing academic achievement as "acting white," they reject peers who do well in school. Though such rejection of institutional norms enables people to stay sane when their world makes little sense, the price is high. They lose hope of creating a service or product that carries their personal signature. They are cut off from using their talents to contribute something of value to the world.

Giving authorship provides space within boundaries. In an orchestra, musicians develop individual parts within the parameters of a particular musical score and the interpretative challenges posed by the conductor. Authorship turns the organizational pyramid not on its head but on its side. Leaders increase their influence and build more productive organizations. Workers experience the satisfactions of creativity, craftsmanship, and a job well done. Gone is the traditional adversarial relationship in which superiors try to increase their control while subordinates resist them at every turn. Trusting people to solve problems generates higher levels of motivation and better solutions. The leader's responsibility is to create conditions that promote authorship. Individuals need to see their work as meaningful and worthwhile, to feel personally accountable for the consequences of their efforts, and to get feedback that lets them know the results.[5]

Under a plant manager who had given the gift of authorship, one autoworker commented, "We make decisions now. Before, we never made no decisions. We just ran the machine and that was it!"

The Gift of Power

The idea of power as a gift may seem paradoxical. Can anyone ever give power to someone else? Would they even if they could? Realists and revolutionaries have long believed that no one but a fool ever gives power away. Power, they argue, must be seized—forced out of the hands of those who hold it. This might be true if giving power to others always meant becoming weaker. Yet Steve's most important lesson at the Topeka plant was that he could give away power and wind up stronger.

The gift Steve offered to the worker with the "half-baked idea" was not like a coin placed in an outstretched hand or a neatly wrapped gift placed under a tree. What Steve offered was an *opportunity* for the worker to empower himself. Like all the other gifts that Maria discussed, the gift of power can only be given to those who want it and are ready to receive it.

Hoarding power produces a powerless organization. Stripped of power, people look for ways to fight back: sabotage, passive resistance, withdrawal, or angry militancy. Giving power liberates energy for more productive use. When people feel a sense of efficacy and an ability to influence their world, they seek to be productive. They direct their energy and intelligence toward making a contribution rather than obstructing progress.

The gift of power enrolls people in working toward a common cause. It also creates difficult choice points, like the one Steve faced when an employee "threw a half-baked idea into the hopper." In such circumstances, if leaders say no and clutch the reins of power too tightly, they reactivate the old patterns of antagonism. If they cave in and say yes to anything, they put the organizational mission at risk. Leaders cannot empower others by disempowering themselves. They need to help others find and make productive use of many sources of power— information, resources, allies, access, and autonomy.[6] The workers and managers who banded together at the Topeka plant tapped many of those sources to gird their recommendations with the clout that made it easy for Steve to say yes.

The gift of power is closely linked to conflict. When power is hoarded and centralized, conflict is often suppressed. Eventually it emerges in coercive or explosive forms. Urban violence provides a contemporary example. Feeling powerless, seeing society as an enemy, young people try to empower themselves through gangs and guns. People who feel genuinely powerful will find more productive options. When a highly centralized system disperses power, the initial outcomes are often surprising and disturbing. Previously hidden conflicts leap to the surface. Interest groups battle for scarce resources. This happened all over Eastern Europe after the collapse of Communism. Effective leadership gives power without undermining the system's integrity, making it possible to confront conflict without warfare and violence. As the psychiatrist and author Scott Peck has observed, "Community is a place where conflict can be resolved without physical or emotional bloodshed and with wisdom as well as grace. A community is a group that fights gracefully."[7]

Authorship and power are related, so the two are easily confused. Autonomy, space, and freedom are at issue in both. Yet there is an important difference. Authorship requires autonomy. Power is the ability to influence others. Artists, scientists, and skilled craftspeople can experience high levels of authorship, even when they work largely by themselves. Power, in contrast, is only meaningful in relationship to others. It is the capacity to influence and get things to happen on a broad scale. Authorship without power is isolating and splintering. Power without authorship can be dysfunctional and oppressive. Each of these two gifts is incomplete. Together, their impact on organizational spirit is extraordinary, a lesson many pioneering companies are beginning to realize.

The Gift of Significance

The Saturn Corporation—General Motors' innovative new automobile maker—is a corporate community that strives to give its employees a coherent sense of meaning and significance. Significance has both internal and external dimensions. The internal dimension is the feeling of unity and cohesiveness that goes with being part of a tightly knit community. The external dimension is the sense of pride associated with contributing something of value to the larger society. Saturn's motto, "A Different Kind of Company, A Different Kind of Car," tries to capture both aspects.

There are potential shadows to tightly knit communities governed by strong ideologies. History holds many examples of supposedly liberating societies that turned out to be oppressive, intolerant, or unjust. Every major religion has seen instances of religious leaders who used spiritual authority for selfish or destructive ends. Parallel risks exist in any group or organization. Community, like love, carries risks of dependence, exploitation, and loss. Yet it makes no more sense to reject community than to shun love and intimacy. We need to approach both with a combination of hope and wisdom.

We build significance through the use of many expressive and symbolic forms: rituals, ceremonies, icons, music, and stories. Humans have always created and used symbols as a foundation for meaning. Organizations without a rich symbolic life become empty and sterile. The magic of special occasions is vital in building significance into collective life. Moments of ecstasy are parentheses that mark life's major passages. Without ritual and ceremony, transitions remain incomplete, a clutter of comings and goings. "Life becomes an endless set of Wednesdays."[8]

When ritual and ceremony are authentic and attuned, they fire the imagination, evoke insight, and touch the heart. Ceremony weaves past, present, and future into life's ongoing tapestry. Ritual helps us to face and comprehend life's everyday shocks, triumphs, and mysteries. Both ritual and ceremony help us experience the unseen webs of significance that tie a community together. However, when inauthentic, such occasions become meaningless, repetitious, and alienating. They waste our time, disconnect us from work, and splinter us from one another. "Community must become more than just gathering the troops, telling the stories, and remembering things past. Community must also be rooted in values that do not fail, values that go beyond the self-aggrandizement of human leaders."[9]

Ceremony and ritual may seem extraordinary and exotic, far removed from the ordinary requirements of life. Yet, while there are grand ceremonies for special occasions, there are also simple rituals that infuse meaning, passion, and purpose into daily routine. Both grand and simple events speak to the soul: "A piece of clothing may be useful, but it may also have special meaning to a theme of the soul. It is worth going to a little trouble to make a dinner a ritual by attending to the symbolic suggestiveness of the food and the way it is presented and eaten. Without this added dimension, which requires some thought, it may seem that life goes on smoothly, but slowly soul is weakened and can make its presence known only in symptoms."[10]

Like ritual and ceremony, narrative is a vessel for soul and spirit. It was difficult for Steve or Maria to talk about significance without the stories that they shared. Stories transport us to the magical realm of spirit.

> Like night dreams, stories often use symbolic language, therefore bypassing the ego and persona and travelling straight to the spirit and soul, who listen for the ancient and universal instructions embedded there. Because of this process, stories can teach, correct errors, lighten the heart and the darkness, provide psychic shelter, assist transformation and heal wounds. . . . The tales people tell one another weave a strong fabric that can warm the coldest emotional or spiritual nights. So the stories that rise up out of the group become, over time, both extremely personal and quite eternal, for they take on a life of their own when told over and over again.[11]

In successful organizations, people's sense of significance is rooted in shared stories, passed from person to person and generation to generation. "Some say that community is based on blood ties, sometimes dictated by choice, sometimes by necessity. And while this is quite true, the immeasurably stronger gravitational field that holds a group together is their stories . . . the common and simple ones they share with one another."[12] These stories are about people, events, triumphs, and tragedies. They transcend time and place. Steve is beginning to understand stories as the symbolic narrative that holds a group together.

In writing this book, we deliberately chose the word *significance* for its dual connotations of meaning and importance. The gift of significance lets people find meaning in work, faith in themselves, confidence in the value of their lives, and hope for the future. Reason and technology often divert our attention from the everyday existential pillars that support our sense of significance. If we lose our gift of fantasy and festival, we lose one of life's most precious gifts. Steve is realizing all this for himself. His next task is to share the gift of significance with others.

Sharing

CHAPTER 12

Summoning the Magic of Stories

He wanted to deny it. He no longer could. She was ill. Too many canceled meetings. Delays in returning calls. Weariness in her voice when she finally did. He was praying with new urgency. Not that he expected prayer to affect her health. It was his heartsong, his way of keeping faith. He'd learned it from her. He hoped she could hear it too.

His eyes rebelled against the harsh sunlight. Heat shimmered from the road ahead. Even with the air-conditioning on full blast, it still felt oppressive. It'll be better in the mountains, he thought. A flood of memories was a welcome distraction. He recalled his first trip up this road. How miserable he felt then. She'd helped him find a way out of hell. Now he understood that spirit is the real life flow. In his life. In his work. Did she know how much she had given? He hoped so.

A note on her door directed him to the back porch. She was napping there. He'd never seen her asleep. He missed seeing her eyes. They were so important to him. Intense. Beacons on his journey. Reflections of his soul.

He sat and waited. Not for long. Somehow, she seemed to sense his presence. She smiled broadly when she saw him. Her usual vitality seemed to return.

Steve, I'm glad you're here. There's lemonade in the refrigerator. Get some glasses and plenty of ice. We need something to cope with the heat.

Compared to the city it's cool.

How's Gwen?

Fantastic! She sends her love.

The wedding was beautiful. I felt your spirit throughout.

You know how much it meant to us to have you there. Gwen loved the poem you read.

'In the sea of love I melt like salt.' I'm glad she liked it.

The other thing that's amazing is that the high I've been on since the wedding is carrying over into work.

You can't compartmentalize spirit.

You remember hearing me talk about Jill Stockton?

Maria frowned momentarily. I think so. She's your financial VP, right?

That's her. Floored me a couple of months ago. Came in with an idea for our next management retreat. Said we should tell stories.

Maria smiled. You were surprised?

Totally. She's good. Brilliant, really. Mostly a number cruncher, though. Funny to hear her suggest we swap stories about the year's highs and lows.

Were you pleased?

Beaming! The best thing is, it's not just her. Things like this are taking off all over the place. Team spirit like I'd always hoped for.

What happened with Jill's idea?

A bunch of people got behind it. They made it the center-piece for our management retreat. We went to this lakeside resort. Beautiful spot. Friday night was the big climax. They'd printed up a fancy program. Billed it as the 'First Annual Lake-side Lore Hour.' All the rules were spelled out in the program.

The rules for what?

For the tournament of tales. Everyone had to share a story at his or her dinner table. About a peak or a valley from the past year. Then each table had to select its best for the finals.

Nominees to compete for the big prize?

Right. In front of the whole group. Even had an applause meter to pick the winner.

Who won?

Would you believe the plant manager in Topeka?

With a story about you, I'll bet.

Remember my side of the story? I thought I'd pulled off one of the great triumphs in modern corporate leadership. His ver-sion was different. What he claimed was the real story behind the story.

How embarrassing was it for you?

Very. As he tells it, I wasn't leading them. They were leading me. They had the whole thing scripted beforehand. They felt sorry for me after I got so beat up. Figured I'd blow it unless I got a lot of help. After I left, they had a party. A big celebration of their victory over the boss. Even gave me an award, except I wasn't there to accept it.

What was the award?

'How to Lead Without Really Trying.'

Even secondhand the story had life. They were both laughing. It felt good.

A great story, she said.

Everyone thought so. People were falling out of their chairs laughing. Their applause pushed the meter off the scale.

How were you feeling?

My stomach was in knots. My jaw was clamped so tight it was pretty hard to smile convincingly.

Did you get to respond?

Required by the rules. I was tempted to set the record straight. But I exhaled, took a deep breath, and decided to go with the flow. Kept it short. Roasting the boss is probably good for the soul anyway. I told them that the stories we shared, even one as outlandish as the winner, were the best gift we could give each other. Together we summoned a common spirit.

How'd they react?

Standing ovation. Not just for me. For everyone there. For our community.

I'm proud of you.

I hoped you would be. You made it possible, you know.

Don't give too much credit to the midwife. You did most of the work yourself. And you felt most of the pain along the way. Give yourself credit.

The sun had begun its descent toward a gap in the mountains. A faint breeze began to stir. They looked at each other. He felt a deep connection, a tenderness he had rarely felt.

He spoke first. His mouth felt dry. A feeling of anguish was growing in his heart. The words were hard to say. I'm feeling pain now.

So am I.

Their eyes met, bridging the silence. He knew what they needed to talk about. Would she volunteer? Should he ask? He didn't have to wait long for her response.

You know I haven't been well.

For a long time, he replied. Did he mean it as a rebuke? He wasn't sure. He'd felt she was avoiding the subject. It bothered him.

Do you wonder why I didn't tell you before?

Friends talk to friends. If you're really so big on giving, why withhold? He hadn't meant to sound so harsh. He saw the flicker of pain in her face and wished he could retract his words.

Her eyes, as bright and intense as ever, never left his. I haven't talked about my health because I hate being a burden for someone I care about. It's easier for me to offer help than take it from others. One of my cardinal imperfections. Anyway, I'm running out of time. You're very important to me. I think of you as a very special legacy.

His anger and guilt had both evaporated. Pushed aside by an overwhelming sense of gratitude and love. That's a big responsibility, he said.

If it's just another burden don't take it.

Not a burden. A gift.

Then enjoy giving it away.

CHAPTER 13

Lifting
Our Voices
in Song

January. Snow flurries falling outside his office window. A tough day ahead of him. Lots of balls in the air. The phone rang. He picked it up.

Is this a good time? she asked.

Perfect, he lied. Thanks for returning my call.

I got your message on the machine. You sounded troubled. What's up? she asked.

A classic blooper. It's not easy to screw up the annual holiday party, he said, But somehow we managed.

That's easier than you think. It's certainly not the first time something intended to be special blew up in someone's face. What happened?

Remember the Lakeside Lore tournament?

How could I forget?

Everyone said it was our best meeting ever. Wonderful feeling of community. Only one problem. Everyone there was senior management. We all felt that we wanted a wider audience, so we could share the feeling with the rest of the corporate staff.

It's a great idea. The problem is pulling it off with the same spirit. Execution is tricky.

We found that out. A group started meeting after the retreat. Called themselves the Lakesiders. They got excited about doing a music video.

Why a music video?

Something to present at our annual holiday fest. You talked about music as a way to express spirit. We produced a musical. Called it 'The Holiday Spirit: Our Way of Life.'

As a special gift for the holidays?

Seemed like a great idea at the time. Everyone at headquarters comes to the party. All the staff. Friends and relations. You can't believe how much work people put into this production.

Making costumes. Rehearsing nights and weekends. Bringing in musicians from the local symphony.

You put a lot into it. How'd it turn out?

Artistically, the tape was fantastic. I thought everyone would love it. Not true. It flopped.

Do you know why?

Good question. I was stunned. I'd introduced the tape myself. Gave it a big buildup. After that it was downhill. No enthusiasm. Embarrassing silence. No laughs at the gag lines. Polite applause at the end. My heart was in my throat.

It sounds awfully painful.

Excruciating. As the video was winding down I said a quick prayer for guidance.

Was your prayer answered?

Got help from somewhere. I was at the podium. Scared to death. Trying to figure out what to say to Kurt.

Who's Kurt?

The corporate CFO. He got wind of the musical. He called to tell me it was a dumb way to spend the company's money. I said, 'Don't worry, we'll get a big return.' He wasn't buying. It's hard to talk spirit to Kurt. He's the kind of guy who'd want numbers on the salvation rate before he'd join a church.

I once had the same feeling about you. Don't write Kurt off too quickly.

At my worst I wasn't as much of a penny-pinching control freak as Kurt.

She said nothing. Over the phone line he couldn't see her raise her eyebrows and roll her eyes. Somehow he knew she had.

Okay, he said. I'll give Kurt the benefit of the doubt.

So continue the story. You're at the podium and the audience is dying on you. What did you do?

Started off by thanking everyone who worked on the video. Then I asked the audience, 'Have you ever watched someone open a gift that you gave them? Then watch them try to hide their disappointment?'

That's a nice analogy.

Seemed to work. I told them you always take a risk when you offer a gift. When it's right, it's glorious. Even if it's not, the same spirit is behind it. That spirit is what our organization is about.

You're getting pretty good at thinking on your feet.

That's because it came from the heart. Thanks to you.

Why was the video the wrong gift?

I'm still wrestling with that.

Start with history. How long has this holiday event been going on?

Years. Way before my time. Same format every year. People thought it needed a little freshening up.

What was the traditional format?

Open bar. Buffet dinner. Holiday talent show. Sopranos. Barbershop quartets. Harmonicas. Magicians. Employee amateur hour. No talent required. Usually went on forever.

What happened to the amateur hour this year?

Gone. Replaced by the video.

You're still wondering why the tape flopped?

He hoped he didn't sound as sheepish as he felt. Guess it's not much of a mystery. We desecrated a time-honored ceremony. Should have seen it coming.

Why didn't you? This is ground you've covered before.

Hubris, maybe. Maybe caught up in the moment. The Lakesiders thought we needed something new. The old format was getting tired. People complained all the time.

Did everyone complain? Who did you hear from?

The Lakesiders, mostly. Big mistake in retrospect. I only talked to the folks who'd already signed on for the new order of service. Most of the audience still liked the old one.

That's an important lesson.

Expensive, too. Silence on the line. Enough of my woes. How are you?

Physically, not so great. Spiritually, excited. Do you know Rumi called death our wedding with eternity?

No, I never heard that. He felt a chill. Losing her was still hard to face.

And I'm making great progress on my book.

Book? You haven't told me...

I've given it a tentative title, *Spirited Leadership*. You'll enjoy it. You're in it.

In the chapter on what not to do?

No. You're featured in the chapter on spiritual development. I just hope I have time to get the book done before...

That's a good incentive to hang around, he said. I have plans for you. Big event coming up in April. I really hope you can come.

What's the occasion?

We're celebrating the company's twenty-fifth anniversary.

I'd love to come. It would be a great honor. But I can't promise anything.

It was not what he wanted to hear.

After saying good-bye he sat in silence for several minutes, watching the snow fall outside his window. He thought back to the time he drove through a blizzard to get to her house. He'd do it again in a moment. Would she make it to April? He wasn't sure.

CHAPTER 14

Celebrating Shared Icons

He was midway through his second cup of coffee. Still basking in memories of the night before. The phone rang. It was Maria. She spoke softly. Her voice was weak, raspy.

I was sorry to miss the anniversary celebration. How was it?

Perfect, except for one thing. You weren't there.

I wanted to be. I just couldn't. Fill me in now. Tell me every-thing.

Well, the Lakesiders kept meeting. They put the plan together.

The holiday party disaster didn't discourage them?

Spurred them on. They were determined to get it right the next time. Involved everyone they could. Set up a bunch of task forces. Amazing what they got done in a couple of months.

Faith moves mountains. Her voice was wavering, but her conviction came through as clearly as ever.

We had some big ones to move. A lot going on. Time crunch. It's tough linking people on four continents. Kurt was on my neck again about wasting money.

Kurt still has faith in the bottom line.

It's his job.

But it all came together?

Barely. The day before launch it looked pretty dicey.

It always does.

The plan was simple. Honor the past. Celebrate the present. Look to the future.

Simple, but elegant. You covered all the bases.

The history group put together an incredible videotape. They had a perfect theme: 'From One Seed, Many Plants.' It opened with John Harding doing a rap song.

John? That's hard to imagine. I've known him since he started the company. He's a wonderful person. But he's a little stiff for rap singing. My voice is pretty much gone, but I might still sing better than John.

He could hear her laughing at the other end. He felt better.

John wasn't too crazy about the costume, either. Plaid shirt. Overalls. Pitchfork. American Gothic. You should have heard him, though. He put his heart into it. In his best scratchy baritone. 'It was back in Cincinnati that we planted the seed. Tried to build a company I'd be proud to lead.'

Unbelievable. It's totally out of character for John. She was laughing even harder. You have to send me a copy of the tape. It could be the best therapy I've had in a long time.

He loved doing it. A vintage performance. Rave reviews.

That's wonderful. He rarely gets that kind of public recognition since he retired.

I owe a lot to John. Without his prodding I'd never have come to see you.

It's a mutual debt. Anyway, what came next?

John finishes his verse. The camera shifts to the chorus behind him. Out steps the original Topeka plant manager to pick up the lyrics. And it went on like that. Our history. Played out right in front of us. Every era and every site. Very moving.

I can't wait to see it.

The audience was mesmerized. They'd all heard of John. A company legend. Most of them had never seen him. Old-timers savored the memories. Newcomers devoured the stories. Everyone loved it.

They usually do. At least when you get the right themes.

Unlike our holiday video. Then it was on to the present. We did this round-the-world televised tour of our facilities. People, places, products. All live with a satellite hookup. Price tag on that one was a tough sell with Kurt. It was worth it. Even he said so later. First time we could all be at the same party. See each other. Talk to each other. Celebrate together. A big family reunion.

John must have been proud.

He was in tears a lot of the time.

Knowing John, that's remarkable.

He wasn't alone. The feelings were so intense. I was just hoping we could make it through the last part.

The future.

Right. We opened with another video. Young people from around the world. Employees and customers. Talking about their dreams—what they hoped we'd become. Powerful, eloquent, inspired stuff. Reminded me how crazy it was to think of myself as the sole source of vision.

You've learned a lot since then. You've developed the courage to let others lead.

I needed more courage than that. I was supposed to close off the event.

The video must have been a tough act to follow.

I was choked up. Couldn't give my prepared speech. Wouldn't have worked anyway. The young people on the tape had said it all.

What did you do?

I talked about you.

You talked about me?

You. I was bone honest. Told them the truth. When I first came into this job I wasn't ready. I didn't know it at the time. John did. He put me in touch with a wise and wonderful person. My spiritual guide. She taught me that leading is giving. That spirit is the core of life. Helped me find my soul. Then I said to the audience, 'All of you have been my teachers as well. Together, we're finding our company's soul. We're building an uncommon spirit. One seed, many plants, a shared dream.'

Silence on the other end of the line. He knew she was crying. So was he.

Thank you, Steve. Thank you very much. It means a lot to me. Be sure to send me the videotape.

INTERLUDE   ✑

Expressing the Spirit

*The most beautiful and profound emotion we can
experience is the sensation of the mystical. It is the
sower of all true science. He to whom this emotion is a
stranger, who can no longer wonder and stand rapt in
awe, is as good as dead. To know that what is
impenetrable to us really exists, manifesting itself as
the highest wisdom and the most radiant beauty, which
our dull faculties can comprehend only in their
primitive forms—this knowledge, this feeling, is the
center of true religion.*

—*Albert Einstein*

We go to services and read prescribed words, not to find God but to find a congregation, to find other people who are in search of the same divine presence as we are. By coming together, singing together, reading the same words together, we overcome the isolation and solitude with which each of us ordinarily lives. We all become one and we create the moment in which God is present.

—*Rabbi Harold Kushner*

Modern managers concentrate mostly on the rational side of enterprise. Neglecting the spiritual dimension they overlook a powerful untapped source of energy and vitality. The costs of this omission are obscured by their deep devotion to the myth that reason can solve all problems. In *Feast of Fools,* Harvey Cox calculates the costs: "Man in his very essence is *homo festivus* and *homo fantasia.* Celebrating and imagining are integral parts of his humanity but western industrial man in the past few centuries has begun to lose his capacity for festivity and fantasy."[1] The loss, says Cox, is personal, social, and religious. It deprives us of a central ingredient of our lives. It makes us provincial and maladaptive. It stills our sense of connection to the cosmos, of contributing to something larger than ourselves.

Steve felt these costs firsthand. They were at the root of his discouragement when he first visited Maria. His life had become flat, dull, and lacking in contour. Devoted to the church of hard work and reason, he paid no attention to his own or his organization's spiritual core. To summon spirit, Steve learned to embrace the symbolic discourse of spirit: art, ritual, stories, music, and icons.

Expressive activity is integral to meaningful human enterprise. Its absence kills faith and hope. People put in time without passion or purpose. Though fictional, the events in the dialogues in this book are based on direct observations of behavior in many successful organizations. Viewed from the outside, expressive events (the pink Cadillacs, diamonds, and other symbols of Mary Kay Cosmetics for example) may appear superficial and hokey. Viewed from the inside, such symbols and ceremonies anchor the organization's soul and release its spirit.

Even newcomers and outsiders can savor the spirit of ceremony. Imagine the feelings of the mechanical engineer who went to pick up his new Saturn automobile and arrived to find it sitting in front of the showroom. As he was handed his keys, all the employees—mechanics, clerks, accountants, custodians—gathered around and sang to him. He said later that he thought he was simply buying a car, but he now felt as if he had joined a family.

Story as Public Dream

In the first dialogue, Steve discovered the magic of stories. Throughout history, people have relied on narrative to express deep spiritual messages hard to communicate any other way. Successful organizations are storied organizations. One does not have to belong to one of them for long or go very far to learn the lore. Many contemporary organizations regularly convene times for storytelling. Over time, layers of story accumulate to help people touch the dream world of corporate mythology. It has been suggested that "a dream is a personal experience of that deep, dark ground that is the support of our conscious lives, and a myth is the society's dream. The myth is the public dream and the dream is the private myth."[2] Without story and myth, there is no public dream. Without shared dreams, organizations falter and perish. Individuals, groups, and organizations all need their own stories. Leaders must venture off the known and protected pathway to find their own private storehouse. Stories help them choose a direction and learn from their experiences. "We tell stories to illuminate the paths we travel, and to share humor, courage and wisdom in this liberation struggle."[3]

Maria's stories provided a temporary beacon on Steve's path to spiritual liberation until he began to spin tales of his own. He was then able to help his company along its own spiritual path. The winning story at the lakeside retreat will take its place in the company's evolving legend. The moral: leaders need followers. The real drive comes from below.

Music as Enhancement

Steve's venture into music as a way to summon spirit provides an important warning. Expressive activity is powerful. When it works, it is majestic. When it goes awry, it can backfire resonantly, leaving in its wake suspicion, feelings of manipulation, and a sense of betrayal. The composers of the ill-fated musical had a good idea. Their effort misfired because they ignored tradition and failed to learn enough about their audience. The resulting performance evoked disappointment and alienation instead of building spirit.

Philosopher Susanne Langer observes that "music is the algebra of feelings."[4] A movie without music is like food without spice or a summer morning without birds singing in the trees. Music is a language of spirit. "It creates magic, consecrates feelings, and stitches together the delicate fabrics of the soul."[5]

Music inspired Steve's epiphany in the Cathedral of Notre Dame. The *a cappella* singing was as essential as the majesty of the setting in creating his powerful spiritual experience. The same power of music is essential in modern organizations. Thomas Watson, Sr., who made International Business Machines one of the most successful companies in the world, understood the importance of singing—IBMers of old sang the company song together. Watson and the song have long since disappeared. Who knows if loss of heart was at the root of IBM's fall from grace in the 1980s?

Walter Durrig, former commander of the Swiss Army, sums it up with a Swiss-German phrase, "*singe oder seckla.*" Roughly translated it says, "either sing or haul ass."

History and Icons

Educational historian Jay Featherstone refers to the U.S. as the "United States of Amnesia," because we have so little appreciation of the significance of history. Without roots, plants perish. Without history, the present makes no sense. Without a historical base, a vision is rootless and doomed. As Steve came to grips with the gift of significance, he realized the vital role of history in the spiritual life of an organization. Celebrations merge past, present, and future into a cohesive symphony. The misguided music video came about because planners ignored company history. In the twenty-fifth anniversary celebration, the planners learned from their prior mistake. As employees around the world reviewed the history of their organization, they strengthened their sense of shared connection and ownership. His-story became *our* story, and that story provided an organic platform for the present and a launching pad for the future.

To summon spirit and care for the soul, we must relearn ancient lessons. There is truth beyond rationality. The bottom line is not the ultimate criterion. There is another dimension. Almost every organization touches this realm from time to time—in retirement parties, holiday gatherings, award banquets, or other special occasions. Too often, such events are last-minute afterthoughts, hastily planned, and half-heartedly attended. People see them as they are: mechanical and spiritless, pale reflections of what they could and should be. Disease of the spirit exacts a high price. Spiritual bankruptcy ultimately leads to economic failure. The deeper cost is a world where everything has a function yet nothing has any meaning.

The symptoms of an undernourished soul appear in countless ways: violence, lethargy, alienation, alcoholism, deterioration of the family. The shrunken modern psyche is "just as much a victim of industrialization as were the bent bodies of those luckless children who were once confined to English factories from dawn to dusk."[6]

A New Life

CHAPTER 15

The Twilight of Leadership

Her call was a surprise. Never before had she called to request a meeting. At first he didn't recognize her voice. Even more disturbing he sensed her real purpose in meeting. She wanted to say good-bye. He tried to lie to himself. Tell himself it was something else. Deep down he knew he had to face the truth.

The familiar road to her house again brought back memories. How nervous he was the first time they met. The time she told him to get lost, and he did. The many times she had turned his questions back to him—keeping his journey alive and on track. He felt nervous again, but for another reason. When they first met, he was desperate about his life. Now he was fearful about hers. As he pulled up the familiar drive, he hoped to see her standing at the doorway. She wasn't there.

He found her sitting in her favorite chair, cloaked in a colorfully embroidered caftan. Her brown eyes seemed even more vivid than he remembered them, her smile both as warm and enigmatic as ever. Then he looked more closely. Her eyes seemed more vital only because her face was so pale and thin. There was a hint of sadness that he had never seen before.

I'm so glad you could come, she said softly.

He knew she was making a noble effort to look strong. Her voice gave her away.

You know I can't stay away for long. He tried to sound upbeat.

Thanks for the videotape. What a wonderful event! I talked to John. He called it a spiritual masterpiece, a work of art. He's very proud. So am I.

You made it possible. Without your . . .

She held up her hand. I didn't ask you here for that. I need to tell you something. I'm running out of time. This is probably it—our last meeting.

He knew it was coming. He still wasn't prepared.

I don't know how long I have, she continued. It isn't much.

I've been trying to convince myself otherwise.

Me too, for as long as I could. Neither of us can deny it any more. I wanted us to have some time together before I go. You're very important to me. More than you'll ever know. I love gardening because I love seeing growth. There's great joy in nourishing something and helping it along. It's a lot like parenting. Your spiritual journey has been a wonderful gift for me.

He made no effort to resist the feelings that surged from somewhere deep inside. You're the parent I never had. Dad died when I was young. I was close to mother, but she was a conscience more than a coach. You've been my guide. You're who I want to become.

Her eyes deepened. Do you remember our first meeting? she asked.

Every minute. I thought about it and all the others on the drive up. How scared I was at first. Feeling the bottom dropping out of my life. Nothing made any sense. Nothing I did made things any better.

That happened to me once. A long time ago. Before you were born. Remember how your career was the only thing that mattered? I was the same way. Maybe even more single-minded. It was tough back then, really tough, for a woman. Top management jobs went to men. I had to be smarter and work harder. It was the only way to get ahead. I made a *lot* of sacrifices.

That's why I touched a nerve when I asked about pictures?

Not just a nerve. You touched my soul. She stopped and closed her eyes. I only fell in love once. Not wisely, but too well. He was married. I got pregnant. I agonized for weeks. My career or my baby?

He had never felt so much empathy for someone else. Nor so much love. His throat tightened. He swallowed hard.

She waited. Then she continued, haltingly. My heart told me to have the baby. My mind said I couldn't keep it. My heart won. He was a boy. Tommy. She stopped and looked down. He could see the tears on her cheeks. He was beautiful. The most wonderful gift I ever received. Then he was gone. SIDS, I guess they'd say now. He's still with me. Every day. He'd be about your age.

Why didn't you tell me? He felt her anguish. He wished he hadn't asked.

She looked down. They sat in silence for several minutes.

At first I didn't make the connection. If I had, I still wouldn't have told you.

Why not?

That wasn't our agreement. You came for spiritual guidance, even if you didn't know it at first. My job was to help you on a journey. Now my journey here is ending. There's more. I want you to know it all. After Tommy's death I tried to lose myself in my career. A lot like you did. I got a chance to start my own business. I was lucky—in the right place at the right time. The business became my child. I put everything into making it a success. It worked—beyond my wildest dreams.

I've heard the stories. You're a legend.

There are other things you don't know. Almost no one does.

Why did you leave your business? Wasn't that like giving your child away?

I got sick. Real sick. I was in a lot of pain. I didn't want anyone to know. It was crazy—the leader isn't supposed to get ill. I started using painkillers. I got more addicted to the pills than to my work. I took a long holiday in Europe. That was the cover story. The truth was I checked into a clinic near Paris. I was looking for medical help. I found more than that. There was a priest there—a very wise man. I've never met anyone with a more ecumenical sense of human spirit. At first he made about as much sense to me as I did to you in our early meetings. But he was patient, and very persistent.

A lot like you.

I hope so. He helped me find a different path.

Like you helped me.

After Tommy's death I'd walled off spiritual questions. The priest showed me that I had to explore them. When I did, I realized they were more real and more important than anything else. He helped me find a new path. I'd already done what I set out to do in business. My company, my second child, was a success. I'd nurtured my successors. I had enough money. I turned over the business to the next generation. I recreated my life around three passions: art, gardening, and spirit.

And helping others. Being a spiritual parent.

That was my new vocation. Helping people along their spiritual paths.

You've helped me find my soul. Challenged me to lead from my heart. Helped me bring spirit to my company. It's a debt I can never repay.

You've already paid in full—with interest.

They sat face to face for several minutes. They didn't need to speak. The silence spoke eloquently—two spirits joined together. Then a sharp pain traveled across her face, breaking the moment.

He knew her store of energy was gone. He wanted to stay. He knew it was time to leave. He walked over and held her hands.

He remembered how comforting her
touch had once been for
him. He hoped it felt as
comforting to her now. She
reached over to the small table
nearby. She handed him a
small envelope. He recognized her
stationery. For later, she said.

Your work will go on, he said,
surprised that it came out as a whisper.

I know. I'll be seeing you.

He barely made it to his car. Biting his lip, he fumbled for his
keys. A rush of tears prevented him from finding the ignition.
He slumped over the steering wheel and cried. Pull yourself
together, he thought. What if she's watching? Then he did the
only thing that made any sense. He took a walk around the lake.

He came to the stream where he and Maria had once
watched a leaf float by. He sat down and opened the envelope.
She had handwritten a short note:

Dear Steve,

More than 400 years ago, the great Italian poet,
Dante, gave poetic form to the journey of his own soul.
He cast Virgil as his guide through the inferno. At the

end of the journey, Virgil takes his leave. Sometimes it's
hard to say what's in our hearts. Virgil's timeless
farewell says what's in mine for you:

> You have seen the fires of passion and hell,
> My son, and now you arrive
> Where I myself can see no further.
> I have brought you here by wit and by art.
> You take as your guide your heart's true pleasure.
> You have passed through the steep and narrow places
> And now the sun shines bright
> upon your brow.
> See around you the flowers and young grasses
> which the soil of paradise grows.
> Your eyes, whose weeping once
> brought me to you,
> now shine far and full of bliss.
> I can go no further.
> Expect from me no further word or sign
> Your feel is right, and sound, and free.
> To disobey it would be a fault.
> Therefore, I give you yourself
> crowned and mitered, you are yours.[1]

A flush of love and pride played against his deep sadness.

CHAPTER 16

Deep Refuge

The funeral was over. He was alone. He knew that. Still, he felt her there. He found himself talking to her. Was he crazy? Talking to a ghost? He didn't care.

He remembered the Saturday evening she died. He and Gwen were spending a rare night alone. Sitting, talking, and touching. Jazz in the background. The doorbell was a surprise. Intrusive, unwelcome. It was John. His face said it all. Maria was dead.

Steve remembered putting his arms around John. They'd never hugged before. You'd have been proud, he said.

He remembered the awkwardness. Gwen taking charge. Getting them into the living room. Pouring wine. Asking them to talk about Maria. Stories. Tears. Laughter. Tears again.

He was talking to her now. As if she were there. At first all I could think about was the void. Who would fill it? How could I go on without you? I didn't think I could. Then I realized your spirit is still here, deep in my heart. It always will be, as long as I keep it alive.

I remember going to your house before the memorial service. Everything still there. The garden. The art. In your bedroom, I found a picture of Tommy. You did keep a photo of someone. Maybe it was enough. I wished Tommy could be there. We could have been friends.

He stopped for a while. Sat in silence. It felt strange to be talking with someone who wasn't there. Why? He remembered what he'd learned from her. He talked to her again. I hope the funeral was what you wanted. Simple. Elegant. From the heart. A reflection of you.

He reviewed in his mind all the stories that her friends had shared. How they came to know her. What she was like. What she had meant to them. Almost everyone there had made their own personal offering. It was John's story that he found himself reviewing and savoring more than any other. He tried to see it all in his mind's eye. A hotel ballroom. A big crowd assembled for a testimonial roast in John's honor. A series of roasters, each more irreverent than the last. Then the MC announcing the evening's featured entertainment—direct from Tokyo, Japan's most revered Kabuki player, Marinari Takehashi. An elegant singer in traditional makeup and full kimono padding gently to center stage. A beautiful voice singing Japanese opera. Marinari bowing deeply and walking over to John. Then, to his complete surprise, jumping in his lap and hugging him enthusiastically. John recoiling in shock. Marinari then whispering in his ear, *Hajimemashite. Gotcha, John-san!* John collapsing in laughter when he finally realized that the great Kabuki singer in his arms was none other than Maria.

The entire service had been a beautiful recollection of an extraordinary person. A unique life that enriched so many others.

He spoke to her again. Maybe you know how much I struggled over what to say. The right words never seemed to come. I'd bought a book of Rumi's poems because you liked them so much. As I read it, the right verse jumped off the page. It said just what I wanted to say. I hope you heard it.

He recited the poem again, slowly:

Three companions for you:
Number one, what you own. He won't even leave the house
for some danger you might be in. He stays inside.
Number two: your good friend. He at least comes to the funeral.
He stands and talks at the graveside. No further.
The third companion, what you do, your work,
goes down into death to be there with you, to help.
Take deep refuge with that companion, beforehand.[1]

After I finished, I looked at faces in the audience. Through my
tears I could see theirs. I knew you were with us.

The Cycle of the Spirit

Clay lies still, but blood's a rover;
Breath's a ware that will not keep.
Up, lad: when the journey's over
There'll be enough time to sleep.

—A. E. Housman

The spiritual cycle has come full circle. In facing Maria's death, Steve begins to anticipate the twilight of his own spiritual journey. Death brings terror. It also brings new life and renewed appreciation for life's gifts. When we wed, we leave one family to join a new one. When we die, we let go of this world to rejoin eternity.

Nuland reminds us how little we control the timing or the manner of our final exit.[1] When it comes, the end is often messy and painful rather than peaceful and dignified. These uncertainties add to the fear and mystery that we experience in the face of mortality. We know that we will die, but continually seek to push this sobering reality into the shadows of consciousness. Ernest Becker wrote that "everything man does in his symbolic world is an attempt to deny and overcome his grotesque fate."[2] The question is whether we must see our fate as grotesque. To deny our destiny is to succumb to fear. To accept it, and to recognize that we contribute through our death as through our life is liberating. It opens new possibilities for life and for leadership.

We usually associate leadership with birth and growth. Rarely do we see much promise in twilight or eclipse. Like all of us, leaders often deny their own mortality and pretend that what they have built will last forever.

An old Sufi tale captures this existential burden. It tells of Jesus walking by a flock of sheep and whispering something in the ear of one. That sheep stops eating and drinking. Several days later Jesus again passes by the flock and asks the shepherd why the one sheep appears to be in such poor health. The shepherd, unaware of to whom he was speaking, replies that someone passed by and whispered something in the sheep's ear. The tale closes with a moral: "If you are curious to know what the venerable Jesus said in the sheep's ear, let me tell you. What the blessed Jesus said was: 'Death exists.' Although it was only an animal, when it heard of death, that sheep stopped eating and went into this state of stupor."[3]

There was a time when Maria's death would have left a gaping wound in Steve's heart and served as a depressing reminder of his own mortality. We all know the feelings of grief and loss that follow the death of someone we love. Steve's spiritual journey opened a new perspective on death. Finding his own soul opened his heart and enabled him to understand that all of us "are continually dying one another's lives and living one another's deaths."[4]

As Steve's personal wounds became an eye to discover his soul, his acceptance of Maria's death opened new possibilities for his leadership. He could now begin each day expecting the unexpected, optimistic that he would find among chaos and

confusion opportunities to shape an enduring human institu-
tion. He could see more clearly how individual efforts can accumulate into a shared historical legacy, knowing that "no matter
what he does, every person on earth plays a central role in the
history of the world. And normally he doesn't know it."[5]

Ernest Becker finds purpose and even optimism in embracing rather than denying death as the end of life's spiritual journey: "The most that any of us can seem to do is to fashion
something—an object or ourselves—and drop it into the confusion, make an offering of it, so to speak, to the life force."[6]

When we succumb to greed, focus only on the bottom line,
and worship exclusively at the altar of rationality, we undermine our search for meaning, passion, and a sense of life's
deeper, spiritual purpose. Steve was fortunate to find a guide
who challenged and encouraged him to search for his own
heart and soul. The search required him to confront deeply the
central questions of meaning and faith: What did he believe?
How did he understand the universe and his place in it? He
faced the central choice point posited by the noted Catholic
theologian Andrew Greeley:

> It seems to me that in the last analysis there are only
> two choices: Macbeth's contention that life is a tale told
> by an idiot, full of sound and fury and signifying

nothing and Pierre Teilhard's "something is afoot in the universe, something that looks like gestation and birth." Either there is plan and purpose—and that plan and purpose can best be expressed by the words "life" and "love"—or we live in a cruel, arbitrary, and deceptive cosmos in which our lives are a brief transition between two oblivions. The data are inconclusive as to these two choices, at least if we look at the data from a rational, scientific standpoint. . . . I opt for hope, not as an irrational choice in the face of the facts, but as a leap of faith in the goodness I have experienced in my life.[7]

As he encountered his soul, Steve made the same decision to opt for hope. He was able to see gifts of leadership as an expression of his faith in life and love, and as a way to help his organization discover a new and vibrant faith. He had become, in theologian Søren Kierkegaard's phrase, a "knight of faith":

This figure is the man who lives in faith, who has given over the meaning of his life to his creator, and who lives centered on the energies of his maker. He accepts whatever happens in this visible dimension without complaint, lives his life as a duty, faces his death without qualms. No pettiness is so petty that it threatens his meaning; no task is too frightening to be beyond his courage. He is fully in the world on its terms and wholly beyond the world in his trust of the invisible dimension. The knight of faith then represents what we call an ordeal of mental health, the continued openness to life out of the death throes of dread.[8]

America's nineteenth-century captains of industry led her organizations to international preeminence. Captains of industry were gradually replaced by modern managers, who have helped us see the virtues of clear goals, measurable objectives, specialization, policy, and accountability. This has taken us a long way from our ancestors, who worked intimately with nature in families and small communities. The challenges of the postmodern era have moved us beyond the reach of both the captains of industry and modern managers. Technological breakthroughs have created previously unknown conveniences and efficiencies. Yet we still face an onslaught of problems that are frustratingly resistant to rational and technical solutions.

More and more of us see that many of those problems are rooted in a disease of the human spirit. President Jimmy Carter may have been ahead of his time when he suggested that the United States was suffering from a spiritual malaise. Few of his countrymen thanked him at the time, but President Bill Clinton returned to the same theme fifteen years later. Nor is this a message restricted to Baptists, southerners, or Democrats. Lee Atwater, one of the architects of President Ronald Reagan's political success, talked about the "spiritual vacuum in the heart of the American society, this tumor of the soul." In another niche of U.S. society, the same message was echoed by a self-described "unemployed, impoverished, chronically-ill, disabled and usually homeless" man in Nashville, Tennessee. He wrote in the editorial page of the local newspaper, "Our nation is having a severe and major spiritual crisis in which the future of the country is in great danger."

To prevail in the face of violence, homelessness, economic depression, and widespread malaise, we need a vision of leadership rooted in the enduring sense of human wisdom, courage, and compassion. We need a new generation of seekers—the Marias and Steves who have the courage to confront their own shadows and to embark upon a personal quest for spirit and heart, and who have the commitment to share their learning with others.

How will we develop the seekers that we need? To begin with, we need a revolution in how we think about leadership and how we develop leaders. Most management and leadership development programs ignore or demean spirit. They desperately need an infusion of poetry, literature, music, art, theater, history, philosophy, dance, and other forms that are full of spirit. Even that would still leave us far short of the cadre of leaders of spirit that we require. Leaders learn most from their experiences—especially from their failures. Too often, though, they miss the lessons. They lack the reflective capacity to learn on their own and have not been fortunate enough to find a spiritual guide, such as Maria, who can help them find their spiritual centers.

In recent decades, we have evolved a kind of implicit compact with the most senior members of our community. In return for better medical care and more financial independence, they are expected to go off to play bridge or golf, leaving the rest of us to get on with our own pursuits. The implicit message is that we want them to be comfortable even though they are largely useless. We have thus cordoned off potential sources of spiritual insight in retirement homes and communities, where their wisdom and experience are rarely available to the rest of us.

Leaders like Steve often find themselves confronting awesome challenges with inadequate reservoirs of experience or seasoning. They look to books, articles, consultants, and workshops and find the latest solution-in-good-standing. When this solution fails, they turn to the next fad. Yet there are countless potential Marias in the world—sources of spiritual guidance who are untapped or underused. A return to spirituality will lead us to seek their wisdom. In matters of spirit, wisdom and experience count far more than technique or strategy.

Like Maria, great spiritual teachers from many cultures and traditions have believed that wisdom comes from within rather than without.

This message is the central point of a story told repeatedly in many different spiritual traditions. The poet and mystic Andrew Harvey offers a Sufi rendition of the tale:

> There was a man who lived in Istanbul, a poor man. One night he dreamed vividly of a very great treasure. In a courtyard, through a door, he saw a pile of blazing jewels heaped by the side of an old man with a beard. In the dream, a voice told him an address, 3 Stassano-poulis Street, Cairo. Because he had learned enough to trust his dream visions, he went on a long arduous journey to 3 Stassanopoulis Street in Cairo. One day, many years later, he came to that doorway, entered through it into a courtyard full of light, saw the old man from his dream sitting on the bench, went up to him, and said, "I had a dream many years ago, and in the dream I saw you sitting exactly where you are

sitting now, and I saw this great heap of treasure by you. I have come to tell you my dream and to claim my treasure." The old man smiled, embraced him, and said, "How strange, I had a dream last night that under a bed in a poor house in Istanbul there was the greatest treasure I have ever seen." At that moment, the poor man saw that what he had been looking for all those years was really under his own bed, in his own heart, at the core of his own life.[9]

The responsibility of the guide is not to give answers, but to raise questions, suggest directions to explore, and to offer support. "Man is reborn, no longer born of the flesh, but reborn of the spirit, of the inspiration from within and the teacher without."[10]

If we look for spiritual guidance, no doubt we can find it. There are many teachers whose wisdom and faith may help us reclaim and regain our hearts, our souls, and our spirit. Our journey is a search, often arduous, for our spiritual center. Once we find our own light within, we can share it with others, offering our own gifts from the heart.

CHAPTER 17 ⁓

The Legacy

A month later Steve was sitting at his desk. Jill Stockton arrived for her two o'clock appointment.

It's your fault, she said. I was fine until you started all this talk about spirit.

So what's the problem?

It always seemed pretty straightforward before. I worked hard in college. Did well in business school. My career is going well. I'm a good financial officer.

One of the best, he said.

My marriage is fine. The kids are great. So why am I starting to ask what's life all about?

A wakeup call. From your soul.

What soul? I don't even know if I have one.

That's the reason for the wakeup call. You find your soul by looking deep within.

How?

Listen to your heart.

What's that supposed to mean?

Your heart is your spiritual center. It's where your soul lives.

And what is my heart supposed to tell me?

I can't tell you what's in your heart. Only you can do that.

He smiled as he remembered his first meeting with Maria. She'd told him the same thing. For everything a season, he thought, and a time for every purpose. Time now to help someone else on their journey.

AFTERWORD:
CONTINUING A SPIRITED DIALOGUE

In this book, we have shared what we have learned from many teachers. There is still much more to learn. We invite readers to participate with us in an ongoing dialogue to deepen our understanding of spirituality.

We know that there are many Steves, Marias, and Jills out there—managers, entrepreneurs, and corporate officers. We would welcome hearing your questions, triumphs and tragedies, hopes and doubts about leadership and spirit at work and in life. If anything in this book touched you, troubled you, or opened new possibilities, please write to tell us. We would also be very interested in hearing about sources and resources for soul and spirit that are meaningful for you. We'll respond and do our best to orchestrate an ongoing conversation. Through shared dialogue, we hope to find new ways to breathe zest and joy into life and work.

You may write to us at the following address:

Lee G. Bolman and Terrence E. Deal

c/o The Jossey-Bass Management Series

Jossey-Bass Inc., Publishers

350 Sansome Street

San Francisco, CA 94104–1310

NOTES

Introduction: Leadership and the Meaning of Life

Epigraph: Rumi, quoted in J. Moyne and C. Barks, *Open Secret: Versions of Rumi* (Putney, Vt.: Threshold Books, 1984), p. 37. Jalal ad-Din ar-Rumi (1207–1273) was a Sufi mystic, poet, and philosopher. Born in Afghanistan, he relocated to what is now a part of modern Turkey after his family was displaced by the Mongol invasion. Sufism is distinguished by its emphasis on religious exercises that produce a direct and personal experience of God. During the tenth through the thirteenth centuries, the ablest thinkers in Islam were often Sufis. Many of them, like Rumi, developed a remarkably inclusive spirituality, not at all consistent with misleading Western stereotypes of Muslims as zealous fundamentalists or backward provincials. Rumi founded the religious order that became known to the West as whirling dervishes because of one aspect of their devotional exercises.

1. M. Gandhi, quoted in A.S.A.A. Al-Suhrawardy, *The Sayings of Muhammad* (Boston: Tuttle, 1992), p. 7.

2. E. Porter, "Notes for Looking for Leadership Conference." Paper prepared for Looking for Leadership Conference at Graduate School of Education, Harvard University, December, 1989, p. 2.

3. V. Havel, "The New Measure of Man," *New York Times*, July 8, 1994, p. A15.

4. T. Moore, *A Blue Fire: Selected Writings by James Hillman.* (New York: HarperCollins, 1991), p. 113.

5. J. Hawley, *Reawakening the Spirit in Work: The Power of Dharmic Management* (San Francisco: Berrett-Koehler, 1993), p. 3.

6. P. L. Berman, *The Search for Meaning: Americans Talk About What They Believe and Why* (New York: Ballantine Books, 1990), pp. 75–83.

7. Berman, *The Search for Meaning*, p. 82.

8. Berman, *The Search for Meaning*, p. 82.

Interlude: Reclaiming Your Soul

Epigraph: Lao-tzu, quoted in S. Mitchell (ed.), *The Enlightened Heart: An Anthology of Sacred Poetry* (New York: HarperCollins, 1989), p. 17. Historians have debated whether Lao-tzu is a historical figure from sixth century B.C.E. China, or whether *Tao-te-Ching*, the work attributed to him, was assembled by others at a later date. Regardless of authorship, the *Tao-te-Ching* is one of the oldest and most durable products of the human spirit.

1. Chuang-tzu, quoted in S. Mitchell (ed.), *The Enlightened Mind: An Anthology of Sacred Prose* (New York: HarperCollins, 1991), p. 20. Chuang-tzu was a Taoist philosopher and teacher who lived in China in the fourth century B.C.E. The quotation is typical of the paradoxes and multiple levels of meaning to be found throughout Chuang-tzu's work. Does he mean that he has said something, but it might not say anything to his reader? Or does he mean that the something he has not said is more important than the something he has? Perhaps it helps to know that he also said, "If the great Way is made clear, it is not the Way."

2. A. Schweitzer, quoted in Berman, *The Search for Meaning*, p. vi.

3. Mitchell's rendering of 1 John 2:27 in *The Enlightened Mind*, p. 32. The *Holy Bible: New Revised Standard Version* gives the same verse as: "As for you, the anointing that you received from him abides in you, and so you do not need anyone to teach you. But his anointing teaches you about all things, and is true and is not a lie, and just as it has taught you, abide in him."

4. Mitchell, *The Enlightened Mind,* p. 209. The novice was Hui-hai, who became a Zen master himself. After Ma-tzu spoke to him, says Hui-hai, "From that day on, I stopped looking elsewhere. All you have to do is look into your own mind; then the marvelous reality will manifest itself at all times" (p. 56).

5. E. Kurtz and K. Ketcham, *The Spirituality of Imperfection: Modern Wisdom from Classic Stories* (New York: Bantam, 1992), p. 35.

6. C. A. Hammerschlag, *The Theft of the Spirit* (New York: Simon & Schuster, 1993), pp. 170–171.

Interlude: Leaning into Your Fear

Epigraph: Lao-tzu, quoted in Mitchell, *The Enlightened Heart,* p. 16.

1. The opening lines of Seng-Ts'an's poem "The Mind of Absolute Trust," quoted in Mitchell, *The Enlightened Heart,* p. 27.

2. W. Blake, quoted in Mitchell, *The Enlightened Heart,* p. 95.

3. Hammerschlag, *The Theft of the Spirit,* p. 50.

4. B. Irwin, quoted in Hammerschlag, *The Theft of the Spirit,* p. 45.

5. Hammerschlag, *The Theft of the Spirit,* p. 45.

6. Kurtz and Ketcham, *The Spirituality of Imperfection,* p. 47.

7. E. Becker, *The Denial of Death* (New York: Free Press, 1975), p. 34.

8. Kurtz and Ketcham, *The Spirituality of Imperfection,* p. 56.

9. J. Campbell (with B. Moyers), *The Power of Myth* (New York: Doubleday, 1988), p. 5.

Interlude: Community and the Cycle of Giving

Epigraph: Rumi, quoted in A. Harvey, *Speaking Flame: Rumi* (Ithaca, N.Y.: Meeramma, 1989), p. 86.

1. C. Pearson, *Awakening the Heroes Within* (San Francisco: HarperSanFrancisco, 1991), p. 1.

2. C. Whitmyer (ed.), *In the Company of Others* (New York: Putnam, 1993), p. 81.

3. T. Moore, *Care of the Soul: A Guide for Cultivating Depth and Sacredness in Everyday Life* (New York: HarperCollins, 1991), p. 77.

4. G. de Borneil, quoted in D. K. Osborne (ed.), *A Joseph Campbell Companion* (New York: HarperCollins, 1991), p. 77.

5. J. R. Hackman, G. R. Oldham, R. Janson, and K. Purdy, "A New Strategy for Job Enrichment." In L. E. Boone and D. D. Bowen, *Great Writings in Management and Organizational Behavior* (New York: Random House, 1987), p. 315.

6. We discuss these and other sources of power in more detail in chapter nine of L. G. Bolman and T. E. Deal, *Reframing Organizations: Artistry, Choice, and Leadership* (San Francisco: Jossey-Bass, 1991).

7. M. S. Peck, *The Different Drum: Community Making & Peace* (New York: Simon & Schuster, 1987), p. 71.

8. D. Campbell, "If I'm in Charge Why is Everyone Laughing?," p. 5. Paper presented at The Center for Creative Leadership, Greensboro, N.C., 1983.

9. E. Griffin, *The Reflective Executive: A Spirituality of Business and Enterprise* (New York: Crossroad, 1993), p. 159.

10. T. Moore, ed., *A Blue Fire: Selected Writings by James Hillman* (New York: HarperCollins, 1991), p. 225.

11. C. P. Estés, *The Gift of Story* (New York: Ballantine, 1993), pp. 28–29.

12. Estés, *The Gift of Story*, pp. 28–29.

Interlude: Expressing the Spirit

Epigraphs: A. Einstein, quoted in Mitchell, *The Enlightened Mind*, p. 191. Rabbi H. Kushner, quoted in P. Berman, *The Courage of Conviction* (New York: Ballantine, 1985), p. 164.

1. H. Cox, *The Feast of Fools* (Cambridge, Mass.: Harvard University Press, 1969), p. 16.

2. Campbell (with Moyers), *The Power of Myth*, p. 48.

3. J. James, "African Philosophy, Theory, and Living Thinkers," in J. James and R. Farmer (eds.), *Spirit, Space and Survival: African American Women in (White) Academe* (New York: Routledge, 1993), p. 31.

4. S. K. Langer, *Philosophy in a New Key* (Cambridge, Mass.: Harvard University Press, 1951), p. xvii.

5. Langer, *Philosophy in a New Key*, p. 236.

6. Cox, *The Feast of Fools*, p. 12.

Fifteen: The Twilight of Leadership

1. Dante Alighieri, *The Divine Comedy*: Purgatory, Canto XXVII. Translated by S. T. Massey in "The Act of Creation and the Process of Learning," keynote address at The Cultural Congress, Indianapolis, Ind., March 12, 1994.

Sixteen: Deep Refuge

1. Rumi, quoted in Moyne and Barks, *Open Secret: Versions of Rumi*, p. 79.

Interlude: The Cycle of the Spirit

Epigraph: A. E. Housman, "Reveille," in A.E Housman, *Last Poems of Alfred Housman* (Boston: Branden Publishing).

1. S. B. Nuland, *How We Die* (New York: Knopf, 1994).

2. Becker, *The Denial of Death*, p. 27.

3. Kurtz and Ketcham, *The Spirituality of Imperfection*, p. 58.

4. N. Frye, in Denham, *Norman Frye: Myth and Metaphor*, p. 224.

5. P. Coehlo, *The Alchemist* (San Francisco: HarperSanFrancisco, 1993), p. 167.

6. Becker, *The Denial of Death*, p. 285.

7. A. Greeley, quoted in Berman, *The Courage of Conviction*, pp. 114–115.

8. S. Kierkegaard, quoted in Becker, *The Denial of Death*, pp. 257–258.

9. A. Harvey, *The Way of Passion* (Berkeley, Calif.: Frog Ltd., 1994), pp. 5–6.

10. G. de Purucker, *Wind of the Spirit* (Pasadena, Calif.: Theosophical University Press, 1984), p. 17.

RECOMMENDED READINGS

Al-Suhrawardy, A.S.A.A. *The Sayings of Muhammad.* Boston: Tuttle, 1992.

Armstrong, K. *A History of God.* New York: Knopf, 1993.

Autry, J. A. *Love and Profit: The Art of Caring Leadership.* New York: Morrow, 1991.

Berman, P. L. *The Courage of Conviction.* New York: Ballantine, 1985.

Berman, P. L. *The Search for Meaning: Americans Talk About What They Believe and Why.* New York: Ballantine, 1990.

Campbell, J. *Hero with a Thousand Faces.* New York: World, 1956.

Campbell, J. *The Power of Myth.* New York: Doubleday, 1988.

Cleary, T. *The Essential Tao: An Initiation into the Heart of Taosim.* San Francisco: HarperSanFrancisco, 1991.

Coelho, P. *The Alchemist.* San Francisco: HarperSanFrancisco, 1993.

Cox, H. *The Feast of Fools.* Cambridge, Mass.: Harvard University Press, 1969.

Estés, C. P. *The Gift of Story.* New York: Ballantine, 1993.

Greenleaf, R. "The Leader as Servant." In C. Whitmyer (ed.), *In the Company of Others.* New York: Putnam, 1993.

Griffin, E. *The Reflective Executive: A Spirituality of Business and Enterprise.* New York: Crossroad, 1993.

Hammerschlag, C. A. *The Theft of the Spirit.* New York: Simon & Schuster, 1993.

Harvey, A. *Speaking Flame: Rumi.* Ithaca, N.Y.: Meeramma, 1989.

Harvey, A. *The Way of Passion*. Berkeley, Calif.: Frog, Ltd., 1994.

Hawking, S. *Black Holes and Baby Universes*. New York: Bantam, 1993.

Hawley, J. *Reawakening the Spirit in Work: The Power of Dharmic Management*. San Francisco: Berrett-Koehler, 1993.

Heider, J. *The Tao of Leadership: Leadership Strategies for a New Age*. New York: Bantam, 1986.

James, J. "African Philosophy, Theory, and Living Thinkers." In J. James and R. Farmer (eds.), *Spirit, Space and Survival: African American Women in (White) Academe*. New York: Routledge, 1993.

Kaplan, A. *Jewish Meditation: A Practical Guide*. New York: Schocken, 1985.

Katz, D. *Just Do It: The Nike Spirit in the Corporate World*. New York: Random House, 1994.

Kidder, T. *The Soul of a New Machine*. Boston: Little Brown, 1981.

Kipnis, A. R. *Knights Without Armor*. New York: Tarcher/Perigree, 1991.

Kurtz, E., and Ketcham, K. *The Spirituality of Imperfection: Modern Wisdom from Classic Stories*. New York: Bantam, 1992.

Kushner, H. *Who Needs God*. New York: Summit, 1989.

Lager, F. *Ben and Jerry's: The Inside Scoop*. New York: Crown Publishers, 1994.

Langer, S. K. *Philosophy in a New Key*. Cambridge, Mass.: Harvard University Press, 1951.

May, R. *The Cry for Myth*. New York: Dell, 1991.

Mitchell, S. (ed.). *The Enlightened Heart: An Anthology of Sacred Poetry*. New York: HarperCollins, 1989.

Mitchell, S. (ed.). *The Enlightened Mind: An Anthology of Sacred Prose*. New York: HarperCollins, 1991.

Moore, T. (ed.). *A Blue Fire: Selected Writings by James Hillman*. New York: HarperCollins, 1991.

Moore, T. *Care of the Soul: A Guide for Cultivating Depth and Sacredness in Everyday Life*. New York: HarperCollins, 1991.

Moyne, J., and Barks, C. *Open Secret: Versions of Rumi*. Putney, Vt.: Threshold Books, 1984.

Needleman, J. *Money and the Meaning of Life*. New York: Doubleday, 1991.

Nuland, S. B. *How We Die*. New York: Knopf, 1994.

Owen, H. *Spirit: Transformation and Development in Organizations*. Potomac, Md.: Abbott, 1987.

Pearson, C. *Awakening the Heroes Within*. San Francisco: HarperSanFrancisco, 1991.

Peck, M. S. *The Different Drum: Community Making and Peace*. New York: Simon and Schuster, 1987.

Peck, M. S. "The Fallacy of Rugged Individualism." In C. Whitmyer (ed.), *In the Company of Others*. New York: Putnam, 1993.

Purucker, G. de. *Wind of the Spirit*. Pasadena, Calif.: Theosophical University Press, 1984.

Shah, I. *Tales of the Dervishes*. New York: Dutton, 1969.

Starhawk. "Celebration: The Spirit of Community." In C. Whitmyer (ed.), *In the Company of Others*. New York: Putnam, 1993.

Terry, R. W. *Authentic Leadership: Courage in Action*. San Francisco: Jossey-Bass, 1993.

Watts, A. W. *The Spirit of Zen: A Way of Life, Work and Art in the Far East*. Boston: Tuttle, 1992.

Whitmyer, C. (ed.). *In the Company of Others*. New York: Putnam, 1993.

Whyte, D. *The Heart Aroused: Poetry and the Preservation of the Soul in Corporate America*. New York: Currency Doubleday, 1994.

ACKNOWLEDGMENTS

Like most books, *Leading with Soul* had its own distinctive genesis. It began at a luncheon in San Francisco with some of our friends at Jossey-Bass. We were discussing potential projects when Lynn Luckow, the president of Jossey-Bass, asked us, "What would you two *really* like to do?" We looked at one another for a while. Out of the ensuing silence an answer somehow emerged: "a book on spirit." (Thanks, Lynn, for being the godparent of this project.)

We left the lunch intrigued—and terrified. Were we qualified to write such a book? We were, after all, social scientists and students of organization. Our formal training in philosophy, theology, and the history of religion was fragmentary at best. As we cast about for a few faint glimmerings of hope, we reminded ourselves that we had written about issues of symbols, meaning, and belief in our earlier works. Also, Terry Deal and Pam Hawkins, of the Vanderbilt Divinity School, had written the paper "Setting the Spirit Free." (Thanks, Pam, for helping us to get going and to take the important step from symbols to spirit.

We thank you for your early guidance. We know that you will be a spiritual guide for many others in the years ahead.)

We went from Jossey-Bass directly to the nearest bookstore. We combed the sections of philosophy, anthropology, poetry, and religion. Each of us carted a dozen or so books back to our hotel. We read and talked, read and talked. Our conversation continued through dinner, all of the next day, and a three-hour airplane trip the day after that. By the time our paths diverged at the Dallas Fort-Worth airport, we had finished the first dialogues and the first interlude. The interlude's original title, "What Did We Just Say?" says all there is to know to about what we were feeling at the time. For the next several weeks, we added and polished, exchanging dozens of drafts between Kansas City and Nashville. With a mixture of fear and hope, we sent a draft of the first section to Bill Hicks and Cedric Crocker, our editors at Jossey-Bass. Though the idea of a pair of male midwives seems faintly incongruous, Bill and Cedric were that and far more for this manuscript. They also enlisted several reviewers, who provided distinctive and very helpful feedback. We cannot thank all the reviewers personally, since most were anonymous, but we did ferret out that Professor Mark Kriger, of the State University of New York at Albany, was the source of a *very* helpful bibliography. (Thanks, Mark, for your generous gift.) Collectively, the reviewers sent a very clear message: this book is worth doing and too important not to do well. The authors are not there yet—and we don't know if they ever will be—but they should keep going. It was just the combination of encouragement and challenge that we needed.

We produced a fuller draft. Our midwives reviewed it and reported that the dialogues sounded strangely as though they had been written by two social scientists. Enter a very discerning fiction editor named Kathy Vian. For a few hours after her feedback arrived, we were seriously demoralized. If she was right—and we both knew she was—we had to write the whole thing all over again. Could we make it over a bar that looked almost insurmountable? Fortunately, along with her feedback, Kathy provided a remarkable short, personalized course in fiction writing.

Recovering from our own brief crisis of spirit, we plunged in anew. The next draft also went to Kathy; she came through again for us. One more push and we were able to deliver the final product. We were then put in the hands of the genially persistent Lasell Whipple, who oversaw the transition from typescript to bound volume with skill and sensitivity.

This book is the product of a real partnership between authors and publisher. Our friends at Jossey-Bass gave us courage and helped us push far beyond where we thought we could go. We can't thank Lynn, Bill, Cedric, Kathy, Lasell, and all their colleagues enough. The finished book is our progeny, but their assistance in a difficult delivery was indispensable.

Homa Aminmadani and her son Behdad reinforced our budding interest in Persian poetry. Behdad also made extensive comments on an early draft. Homa and Deborah Hoskins provided indispensable logistical and personal support. Donna Culver provided friendship and support, and introduced us to a number of contemporary spiritual works. A number of friends and colleagues commented on early versions of the manuscript. Linda French, a corporate lawyer with soul, gave generously of her time and insights. We also received very insightful suggestions from two versatile and spirited physicians, Drs. Rich Davis and Bowen White.

Susan Sonnenday Vogel and Lovett Weems of the Saint Paul School of Theology, John Weston of All Souls Unitarian Universalist Church in Kansas City, and Joseph Hough of Vanderbilt Divinity School all gave us very helpful and incisive comments based on their deep understanding of both theology and leadership. Cheryl Lison, Brad Bates, and Gerry DiNardo, head football coach at Vanderbilt, provided many helpful substantive and editorial comments. Bob and Linda Leftwich provided feedback that combined the pragmatic perspective of a corporate executive with the sensitivity of a clinical psychologist. Nashville radio personality Teddy Bart, and Vanderbilt colleagues Casey Bayluss, Wendy Smith, Jackie Shrago, and Brad Gray provided much-appreciated confirmation that we were on the right track, as did many other people who were present at some of our early efforts to talk about leadership and spirit. Linton Deck and Linda Martinez provided helpful critiques of our final draft. We thank all of them for their counsel and support.

Naoto Sasaki of Tsukuba University contributed important insights about the role of spirit in Japanese management. We are also grateful to Dr. Michael Maccoby for his thoughts on love and the disciplines of the heart. Bill O'Brien exemplifies the kind of spirited leadership we have tried to write about, and we appreciate his support. Ed and Beth Smith provided encouragement, friendship, and wise counsel. Dave Brown, Tim Hall, Bill Kahn, Phil Mirvis, and Barry Oshry of the Brookline Circle helped pave the way for this book through many years of spiritual sustenance.

All our children have contributed to our spiritual journeys. Janie Deal exemplifies in her social work career the kind of spunk that we are writing about. Chris Bolman's penetrating question (quoted in the Introduction) about his father's qualifications for this work was perfectly timed. Brad Bolman's unexpected attachment to Terry Deal's idiosyncrasies ("Terry wacky," Brad always says, with two-year-old confidence and exuberance) was a delightful source of energy and enlightenment. Edward Bolman's contribution to this book was as profound as it was paradoxical. Shelley Bolman brings to his father the joys of a child who has become a very good friend. Lori Bolman's gift of love and caring is appreciated more with each passing year. Scott Bolman's humor and intellectual integrity contributed to the story we tell here.

As always, our wives, Sandy Deal and Joan Gallos, played an integral role in our effort. Each was remarkably tolerant of the other's husband as a frequent houseguest. Sandy was an indispensable supportive presence as we struggled to rebuild our morale after midpoint reviews made it clear how much further we had to go. Joan was a tireless source of questions, ideas, suggestions, and new readings on spirituality. Joan and Sandy provided an environment of love and support that made it both possible and worthwhile for us to keep going.

Our search for traditional sources of spiritual wisdom brought a new appreciation for all that our parents did to make us and our work possible. Florence and Eldred Bolman and

ACKNOWLEDGMENTS

Robert and Dorothy Deal helped us early in our lives to develop an appreciation for the world of spirit. Though it may have taken longer than they hoped for the fruits of their labor to mature, their influence is evident throughout.

For the two of us, this book was another step on our joint journey to wherever our collaboration will take us, even though that step was not in a direction either of us had anticipated. Once embarked, we had to reach deeply into our individual and shared spiritual lives, and our journey continues to deepen our understanding of life's most important treasures. We hope *Leading with Soul* will encourage others to reach out and explore life's mystery and magic, to touch with awe the depths of soul and the peaks of spirit, and to see life as a gift and leadership as a process of giving from one's heart.

THE AUTHORS

LEE BOLMAN is an author, teacher, and consultant. His earlier work on organizational leadership awakened his interest in the spiritual underpinnings of life at work. Born in Brooklyn, New York, to midwestern parents, he has journeyed physically and spiritually between east and west ever since. Along the way, he earned a B.A. in history and a Ph.D. in organizational behavior at Yale. He currently holds the Marion Bloch Chair in Leadership at the University of Missouri-Kansas City. Lee has been a consultant to corporations, public agencies, universities, and public schools all over the world.

He lives in Kansas City, Missouri, with his wife, Joan Gallos, and the two youngest of his six children.

TERRY DEAL is an author, teacher, and consultant. His fascination with the symbolic side of modern organizations led to the publication of the best-selling *Corporate Cultures* (1983, with A. A. Kennedy). His most recent publications include *Managing the Hidden Organization* (1994, with W. A. Jenkins). His current explorations of the world of spirit evolved from his earlier interest in the role symbols play in contemporary organizations. Terry holds a B.A. in history from the University of LaVerne, an M.A. in educational administration from California State University at Los Angeles, and a Ph.D. in education and sociology from Stanford University. He is now a professor in education at Vanderbilt's Peabody College and a consultant to business, health care, military, educational, and religious organizations both inside and outside the United States.

He lives on a mountaintop in Nashville, Tennessee with his wife, Sandy, and their cat, Sam.

Bolman and Deal first met in 1976 when they were assigned to co-teach a course on organizations in the same Harvard University classroom. Trained in different disciplines on opposite coasts, they disagreed on almost everything. It was the beginning of a challenging but very productive partnership. They have written five other books together, including *Reframing Organizations: Artistry, Choice, and Leadership* (Jossey-Bass, 1994).

This page constitutes a continuation of the copyright page.

Brief quotes from *Tao Te Ching* by Stephen Mitchell are reprinted by permission of HarperCollins Publishers, Inc. Copyright (c) 1988 by Stephen Mitchell.

Brief quotes from *The Enlightened Mind* by Stephen Mitchell are reprinted by permission of HarperCollins Publishers, Inc. Copyright (c) 1991 by Stephen Mitchell.

Poetry by Rumi from *Speaking Flame: Rumi* by A. Harvey is reprinted by permission of Meeramma Publishers.

Poetry by Rumi from *Open Secret: Versions of Rumi* by J. Moyne and C. Barks is reprinted by permission of Threshold Books.

Poetry from *Last Poems of Alfred Housman* by A. E. Housman is reprinted by permission of Branden Publishing Boston.

Quote from *Courage of Conviction* by P. L. Berman is reprinted by permission of Ballantine, a division of Random House, Inc.